# CONSTELLATIONS

Like the future itself, the imaginative possibilities of science fiction are limitless. And the very development of cinema is inextricably linked to the genre, which, from the earliest depictions of space travel and the robots of silent cinema to the immersive 3D wonders of contemporary blockbusters, has continually pushed at the boundaries. **Constellations** provides a unique opportunity for writers to share their passion for science fiction cinema in a book-length format, each title devoted to a significant film from the genre. Writers place their chosen film in a variety of contexts – generic, institutional, social, historical – enabling **Constellations** to map the terrain of science fiction cinema from the past to the present... and the future.

> 'This stunning, sharp series of books fills a real need for authoritative, compact studies of key science fiction films. Written in a direct and accessible style by some of the top critics in the field, brilliantly designed, lavishly illustrated and set in a very modern typeface that really shows off the text to best advantage, the volumes in the **Constellations** series promise to set the standard for SF film studies in the 21st century.'
> **Wheeler Winston Dixon, Ryan Professor of Film Studies, University of Nebraska**

 Constellations

 Constelbooks

## Also available in this series

*12 Monkeys* Susanne Kord

*Blade Runner* Sean Redmond

*Brainstorm* Joseph Maddrey

*Children of Men* Dan Dinello

*Close Encounters of the Third Kind* Jon Towlson

*The Damned* Nick Riddle

*Dune* Christian McCrea

*Ex Machina* Joshua Grimm

*Inception* David Carter

*Mad Max* Martyn Conterio

*RoboCop* Omar Ahmed

*Rollerball* Andrew Nette

## Forthcoming

*Lost* Brigid Cherry

*The OA* David Sweeney

*Seconds* Jez Conolly & Emma Westwood

*Stalker* Jon Hoel

*The Stepford Wives* Samantha Lindop

# CONSTELLATIONS

## Jurassic Park

Paul Bullock

## Acknowledgements

Thanks to John Atkinson at Auteur/LUP for the support, insight and opportunity to live a dream and write about the film that first got me excited about cinema. I couldn't have done this without my family; Mum, Dad, Gemma, Steven, James, and the next generation of Jurassic enthusiasts, Nate and Wyatt. Thanks too to my friends – Stephen O'Malley, Gemma Duggleby, Jack Hirst, Carla González, Joana Ferreira, Poppy Ingham and Richard Farrow – who've had to listen to me talk about dinosaurs more than anyone should.

## Dedication

For Mum and Dad & Nate and Wyatt

First published in 2020 by
Auteur, an imprint of Liverpool University Press,
4 Cambridge Street, Liverpool L69 7ZU
www.liverpooluniversitypress.co.uk/imprints/Auteur/
Copyright © Auteur 2020

Series design: Nikki Hamlett at Cassels Design
Set by Cassels Design www.casselsdesign.co.uk
Printed and bound in Poland by BooksFactory.co.uk

All rights reserved. No part of this publication may be reproduced in any material form (including photocopying or storing in any medium by electronic means and whether or not transiently or incidentally to some other use of this publication) without the permission of the copyright owner.

British Library Cataloguing-in-Publication Data
A catalogue record for this book is available from the British Library

ISBN paperback: 978-1-9993340-4-8
ISBN hardback: 978-1-80034-832-5
ISBN ebook: 978-1-80034-764-9

# Contents

INTRODUCTION: A BUTTERFLY FLAPS ITS WINGS ......................................................... 7
(Not) Defining Science Fiction
Spielberg and Genre
*Jurassic Park* and Genre
Reading *Jurassic Park*
Synopsis

CHAPTER 1: ADVENTURES ON EARTH ......................................................... 23
The Green World
Dinosaurs Rule the Earth
Debug the System
Life Finds a Way

CHAPTER 2: LIFE THROUGH A LENS ......................................................... 45
Spielbergian Reality
Silver Screens and Spielberg Faces
I'll Show You
Something Real

CHAPTER 3: DINOSAURS EAT MAN ......................................................... 63
The Spielberg Man
Chaos and Control
Sheer Will
Evolution

CONCLUSION: RAIN INSTEAD OF SHINE ......................................................... 83
These Violent Delights
Kings of the Monsters

WORKS CITED ......................................................... 95

# INTRODUCTION: A BUTTERFLY FLAPS ITS WINGS

An author sits at his desk and clacks his typewriter keys and in Hollywood a director loads his camera with film. Fate? Coincidence? Chaos? Whatever it was, there was certainly something at play in the involvement of Steven Spielberg in the cinematic adaptation of Michael Crichton's 1990 novel *Jurassic Park*. Judging by his work in the few years prior to its release, the film should never have happened. With Holocaust drama *Schindler's List* (1993) on his mind and eventually released in the same year as his dinosaur epic, Spielberg had, since the mid-to-late 1980s, started distancing himself from blockbusters. That kind of filmmaking was frustrating him, and while he had successfully returned to the genre with *Indiana Jones and the Last Crusade* (1989), his most recent relapse (1991's *Hook*) was a critical disaster that he still regrets. 'I'm hoping someday I'll see it again and perhaps like some of it,' he told the BBC in 2013.

When he first heard of *Jurassic Park*, Spielberg was meeting with Crichton to discuss an entirely different project: a TV medical drama that would eventually become the hugely successful *E.R.* (1994-2009). The conversation turned to Crichton's other projects, and he mentioned that he had recently completed a novel about a theme park populated by bioengineered dinosaurs. The idea piqued Spielberg's interest. 'You know, I've had a fascination with dinosaurs all my life,' he told Crichton. 'I'd really love to read it' (Shay and Duncan, 1993: 6). Crichton gave Spielberg a copy of the galleys, and a path was set. Despite interest from Spielberg's Amblin protégé Joe Dante and a Tim Burton hot off *Batman* (1989), Spielberg was announced as director in May 1990 and the film arrived three years later, ushering in a new era of cinematic special effects and breaking box-office records along the way.

*Jurassic Park* occupies an unusual position in Spielberg's body of work, being both highly celebrated and somewhat overlooked. Having spawned four sequels (to date), a number of video games and several comic book series, the film has won the passionate and devoted fanbase that goes with most modern Hollywood franchises. These fans hold the film dear, and have set up online communities to celebrate every aspect of its production and legacy. This passion extends to the movie-going public

*Figure 1: Steven Spielberg released* Jurassic Park *at a key turning point in his career. (© Universal Pictures / Amblin Entertainment)*

as a whole, and in 2015 and 2017 it was voted as one of the top 20 films of all time in two separate *Empire* magazine readers' polls. A 3D re-release in 2013 further swelled the initial box office to a total $1.02 billion, while the overwhelming success of the fourth film, *Jurassic World* (which made $1.6 billion), marked the franchise's triumphant return to the big screen in 2015. Even in a cinematic landscape dominated by superheroes, the public still seems to hold an enduring fascination with all things Jurassic.

The affection is not quite shared by the critical community. Though it received generally positive reviews upon release, *Jurassic Park* was deemed stronger in realising its animal characters than their human counterparts. The New York Times' Janet Maslin wrote that Spielberg 'has taken the bite out of this story' by 'sweetening the human characters, eradicating most of their evil motives and dispensing with a dinosaur-bombing ending [seen in the novel]... Luckily, this film's most interesting characters have teeth to spare' (Maslin, 1993). Variety's Todd McCarthy agreed, adding that while *Jurassic Park* may be 'one-dimensional and even clunky in story and characterisation... it definitely delivers where it counts, in excitement, suspense and the stupendous realisation of giant prehistoric reptiles' (McCarthy, 1993). Fun, but dumb seemed to be the consensus, with Adam Mars-Jones' review for The Independent arguing that even when placed alongside its genre counterparts, *Jurassic Park* still falls flat intellectually:

# Jurassic Park

The cultural lineage of *Jurassic Park* runs through *King Kong* to *Frankenstein*, and the film dutifully includes debates, in advance of disaster, about the morality of bringing the dinosaurs back to life for profit. But it never really convinces as a film preoccupied with worries about nature or science or commerce or all three. Spielberg is too much in love with the beasties he can conjure up to moralise in more than a token way about the legitimacy of their presence out of their time. (Mars-Jones, 1993)

Seen through these criticisms, *Jurassic Park* is something of a regressive anomaly in Spielberg's career. His turn away from blockbusters during the mid-to-late 80s had been a result of his frustration at being dismissed as a simple audience-pleasing entertainer. The films he made – *The Color Purple* (1985) and *Empire of the Sun* (1987) – are disturbing incursions into the dark side of human nature that act as determined bids to change how he was judged and his films were viewed. The man who was accused of pandering to the audience's every whim in *Jaws* (1975), *Close Encounters of the Third Kind* (1977) and *E.T. The Extra-Terrestrial* (1982) decided that, 'God, maybe I should please a part of me I haven't pleased before... a side that doesn't necessarily think of the audience with every thought and breath, but thinks about what I need to be satisfied.' (Forsberg in Friedman and Notbohm, 2000: 127). He 'didn't want to make another movie that dwarfs the characters' (Collins in Friedman and Notbohm, 2000: 122) and was aiming for projects that would allow him to 'challenge myself with something that was not stereotypically a Spielberg movie' (ibid., 121).

Even the films that were 'stereotypically a Spielberg movie' reflected a more ambiguous director. *Raiders of the Lost Ark* (1981) positions its lead as a dark and shadowy figure and compares the power of cinema to the power of the Ark: a dangerous force that must be respected and will punish those who fail to do so. Sequel/prequel *Indiana Jones and the Temple of Doom* (1984) is bigger and brasher than its predecessor and throws Indy into such dark territory that it helped inspire the Motion Picture Association of America to create a new certification for younger viewers: the PG-13. Meanwhile, *Last Crusade* goes to great lengths to mock and undercut its hero. Indy is subjected to humiliating physical comedy (he is struck across the head with a vase), on the receiving end of withering glares from his father who disapproves of his violence, and seen to make assertions to his class ('... X never, ever marks the spot') that are proven to be inaccurate – a critical clue on the journey to locating the Holy Grail is found under a gigantic black 'X' in the middle of a Venice library.

The extended sunset horseback ride that concludes *Last Crusade* is both a loving homage to the Westerns Spielberg enjoyed as a boy and a melancholic farewell to the traditional filmmaking styles and simple pleasures those movies (and the three Indy films) represent. 'I feel as if I've graduated from the college of Cliffhanger U,' (Corliss, 1989) he said in press for the film, echoing his insistence to the New York Times a year earlier that he's 'up to here with I don't want to grow up' (Forsberg in Friedman and Notbohm, 2000: 130). Both personally and professionally, Spielberg was evolving, so why direct *Jurassic Park*? Why regress with a film that posed no great challenge and no obvious opportunity for artistic or personal development: the kind of film he seemed to have spent the final years of the 80s trying to distance himself from? To begin our understanding, it is necessary to look at the genre it is a part of, the impossibility of defining it and how Spielberg made that work in his favour.

## (NOT) DEFINING SCIENCE FICTION

For a genre that has spawned some of the most popular films of all time, science fiction is surprisingly difficult to define. Perhaps the most obvious place to start is with its fantastical elements. One of the core reasons the genre is so beloved is that it takes us beyond the boundaries of the real world and into somewhere entirely different. Before the birth of cinema, when sci-fi was still in its literary form, this unbridled imagination helped it gain traction, and as movies have developed, filmmakers have been able to craft incredible worlds populated by fantastical creatures, breathtaking landscapes and mind-bending technology, developing the most cutting edge special effects to do so. In response, audiences have flocked to the cinema in their droves, eager to witness Maria in *Metropolis* (1927), lunar landscapes in *Destination Moon* (1950), thrilling space battles in *Star Wars* (1977) and the floating mountains of Pandora in *Avatar* (2009). We love science fiction because it takes us where no other genre, and indeed life itself, can.

This approach clearly identifies some obvious examples of sci-fi, such as *2001: A Space Odyssey* (1968) and *The Matrix* (1999), but what about films that do not take place in fantastical locations, feature alien creatures or show off advanced technologies? Stanley Kubrick's *Dr Strangelove* (1964) and *A Clockwork Orange* (1971) are set in very real and relatable worlds, but clearly have science fiction elements to them. The same can be said of *The Truman Show* (1998), *Eternal Sunshine of the Spotless Mind* (2004) and *Melancholia* (2011). Are they less a part of the science fiction genre than *2001* simply because they exist in a recognisable reality?

Perhaps a more rigorous approach is in order, and we need to scratch beneath the surface to look at something less tangible: philosophies and themes. In a letter dated 14 May 1981, one of the genre's leading literary practitioners, Philip K. Dick, considers numerous ways to categorise science fiction and ultimately offers the insight of California State University professor Dr. Willis McNelly, who, Dick notes, 'put it best when he said that the true protagonist of an sf story or novel is an idea and not a person' (Dick, 1990). The films I've mentioned so far certainly support this assertion, but so too do many other films that we would not, or would not easily, attribute to the sci-fi genre. Does the high fantasy of George R.R. Martin's *Game of Thrones* not ask questions about the nature of man and our taste for self-destruction in pursuit of power? Does a fairy tale like 'Hansel and Gretel' not tap into the child's fear of strangers and the dread of the unknown? Does *Alien* (1979), which so effortlessly blends science fiction and horror, not comment on sexuality and male rape?

Perhaps focusing purely on scientific and technological ideas will help us more clearly identify the genre? Maria Pramaggiore and Tom Wallis (2005) argue that science fiction revolves around the relationship between humanity and technology:

> ...science fiction films explore the potential of human ingenuity and ponder the spiritual, intellectual, and/or physical costs of technological development. They suggest that technology alone is impotent, or worse, destructive, unless its development coincides with an expansion in the human capacity for creativity, empathy, and/or humility. (Pramaggiore and Wallis, 2005: 354)

This establishes the genre's critical theme, but Pramaggiore and Wallis go on to identify a number of connected sub-genres that touch on that theme in different ways: exploration films, invader films, mad scientist films and dystopian films. They also note that it is 'difficult to discern' the difference between sci-fi and its close genre cousin horror. With the likes of *Demon Seed* (1977), *Videodrome* (1983) and *Splice* (2009) all locating the source of their terror in technology this is certainly true, but there are further links with other genres and storytelling forms as well. Comic book heroes such as Spider-Man, The Incredible Hulk and Iron Man find their origins in the intersection of humanity and technology, and film adaptations have remained true to those roots. Meanwhile, J.R.R. Tolkein's *The Lord of the Rings* (1954/5) explores mechanisation and industrialisation, and even certain James Bond films (notably *Moonraker* (1979) and *Tomorrow Never Dies* (1997)) have links with the genre too. All these films discuss science, technology and our application of them – but are they science fiction, either partly or wholly?

When it comes to categorising science fiction, no definition is entirely wrong, but no definition is entirely right either. Perhaps the idea of being right at all when defining sci-fi is impossible and even *attempting* to do so is inherently reductive – to sci-fi specifically and genre studies as a whole. Science fiction is not *just* about science, technology or ideas; it is not just about one thing at all. It exists on a wide and diverse spectrum and can have blended into its DNA the Western (*Westworld*, 1973)), the horror film (*The Fly*, 1986), the family drama (the *Back to the Future* series, 1985-89), the teen film (*War Games*, 1983), the epic myth (the ongoing *Star Wars* series, 1977- ) and even the comedic (*Sleeper*, 1973). All of these films, and many more genre-blenders besides, are undoubtedly science fiction, but they are not *just* science fiction, and that very elasticity is precisely what makes the genre so unique. As Paul Kincaid put it in his essay 'On the Origin of Genre',

> ...science fiction is not one thing. Rather it is any number of things – a future setting, a marvellous device, an ideal society, an alien creature, a twist in time, an interstellar journey, a satirical perspective, a particular approach to the matter of the story, whatever we are looking for when we look for science fiction, here more overt, here more subtle – which are braided together in an endless variety of combinations. (Kincaid in Gunn and Candelaria, 2005: 50)

## SPIELBERG AND GENRE

With these combinations in mind, the genre's appeal to Steven Spielberg is clearer. An eclectic filmmaker, he has been playing with storytelling forms since his very early days. Amateur efforts saw him jump between science fiction (*Firelight*, 1964), war movies (*Escape to Nowhere*, 1961) and Westerns (*The Last Gun*, 1959) as he experimented while finding his voice. This continued when he turned professional and moved into television, where he made horrors, detective stories and legal dramas in the shape of *Something Evil* (1972), Columbo pilot episode 'Murder by the Book' (1971), and *Owen Marshall, Counselor at Law* episode 'Eulogy for a Wide Receiver' (1971) respectively. Before his first second of celluloid had flickered its way across a cinema screen, Spielberg delighted in defying genre boundaries.

Five decades on, nothing has changed. Now over thirty features deep, the Spielberg back catalogue covers Cold War thrillers (*Bridge of Spies*, 2015) and animated romps (*The Adventures of Tintin: The Secret of the Unicorn*, 2011); comedies (*1941*, 1979) and fantasies (*The BFG*, 2016); con capers (*Catch Me If You Can*, 2002) and weighty biopics (*Lincoln*, 2012). He has shown a remarkable dexterity in his output and even within these genres, he has experimented. *Jaws* mixes together elements of the horror movie and the post-Watergate political drama, while *The Terminal* (2004) is a light romantic comedy that, in the words of Empire's Ian Nathan, '[channels] both Capra and Kafka'. (Nathan, 2004)

They may demand a more rigid adherence to fact, but his historical dramas merge storytelling modes as well. *Empire of the Sun* incorporates elements of magical-realism as Spielberg shows his young hero coping with the horror of war through fantasy, while critic Andrew M. Gordon has described *The Color Purple* as 'a Cinderella story' (2008: 2). Speaking in 2015 during promotion for *Bridge of Spies*, Spielberg told Australia's ABC News that he relishes this kind of diversity: 'There's something to say about filling our lives with a kind of eclectic variety that gives us a chance to jump in and out of different genres without having to poo-poo a genre because, "I'd never go there, I'm too good for that". I love making movies that are so different from other movies I've made. I enjoy the variety more than anything else.'

Yet Spielberg repeatedly returns to – and remains deeply embedded within – one genre in particular: science fiction. At least eight of his films can be confidently classed as sci-fi – *Close Encounters*, *E.T.*, *Jurassic Park*, *The Lost World: Jurassic Park* (1997), *A.I. Artificial Intelligence* (2001), *Minority Report* (2002), *War of the Worlds* (2005) and *Ready Player One* (2018) – and he has accrued a number of sci-fi based credits in his role as a producer: the *Back to the Future* trilogy, *\*batteries not included* (1987) and the *Men in Black* series (1997– ) in film, and *Amazing Stories* (1985-87), *SeaQuest DSV* (1993-96) and *Falling Skies* (2011-15) on television, to name but a few. The association persists, in part, because many of his most indelible images have come within the genre – the Mothership descending on Devil's Tower, E.T. and Elliott flying across the face of the moon – but it also speaks to the genre itself and how its elasticity and indefinability allow Spielberg to be even more resistant to genre boundaries.

When Spielberg makes a sci-fi film, he is bolder in adding elements we would not typically associate with the genre. *A.I.* riffs on *Pinocchio* (1940) to create a family-based science fiction fairy tale that comments on the Holocaust and environmental issues. *Minority Report* blends film noir with modern blockbuster stylings and the Hitchcockian thriller in what Spielberg dubbed 'a gourmet popcorn movie' (Dubner in Friedman and Notbohm, 2000: 238). *War of the Worlds*, meanwhile, is a divorce drama that incorporates flavours from the disaster and horror genres to comment on the trauma of post-9/11 America. This is not just a new phenomenon; he has been introducing other genres into sci-fi since his early years. Like *Jaws*, *Close Encounters* and *E.T.* reflect post-Watergate American paranoia, but they are also positioned as domestic soap operas and perhaps even as fairy tales too – *Close Encounters* references *Pinocchio* as explicitly as *A.I.* does, even going so far as to quote 'When You Wish Upon A Star'. Would these films have worked so well if they were pure dramas or 'just' sci-fis; if Roy Neary had pursued his dream of forming a band, for example, or Elliott had travelled to E.T.'s planet instead of E.T. to Earth?

It is difficult to say for sure either way, but what is clear is that Roy having his first alien encounter while marooned in his truck and Elliott and E.T. flying across the face of the moon on their bike are so indelible because of the way Spielberg uses sci-fi as a melting pot of ideas, tones, textures and possibilities. Making these movies in any other genre, or focusing on science fiction as a genre purely of technology and fantasy, would have limited him and could have diminished his films' impacts. So, when he approached 1993 and the seminal moment in his career that the year represents, it is perhaps no surprise that one of the two movies he chose to release was a science fiction film. While *Schindler's List* required adherence to fact and a straight-laced, realistic approach, *Jurassic Park* offered the opportunity for imagination and invention. It was an opportunity Spielberg grasped with both hands.

## *JURASSIC PARK* AND GENRE

Taking Dick's definition of science fiction as a genre of ideas, *Jurassic Park* is, at its core, a science fiction film; indeed, prior to *A.I.* and *Minority Report*, it was arguably Spielberg's 'hardest' science fiction film, focusing as it does on the way science is applied and abused. Quoted in a 1993 article by the New York Times, Crichton said the book addresses some of his concerns about 'scientism', which he saw as an 'unthinking acceptance of scientific ideas' (Browne, 1993). Speaking in Starburst magazine, Crichton added:

> I believe that science is a wonderfully powerful, but distinctly limited tool. You decide you'll control Nature, and from that moment on you're in deep trouble, because you can't do it. You can make a boat, but you can't make the ocean. You can make an airplane, but you can't make the air. Your powers are much less than your dreams would have you believe. (1993: 11)

Spielberg echoed these worries. 'Every gain in science involves an equal and opposite reaction – a loss, usually a loss of the environment,' he told the New York Times. 'Science is intrusive. I wouldn't ban molecular biology altogether, because it's useful in finding cures for AIDS, cancer and other diseases. But it's also dangerous, and that's the theme of *Jurassic Park*.' (Browne, 1993)

So effective is the film at communicating its themes that it has become a part of real-life scientific dialogue. Upon release, the long-running American TV programme *Nova* (1974– ) dedicated an episode to the prospect of bio-engineering technology becoming a reality ('The Real Jurassic Park'), and when cloning is discussed in the media, it is often done with a reference to Spielberg's film. *'Is Jurassic Park about to become reality? Scientists "CLOSER" to bringing dinosaurs back,'* wrote the Daily Express in 2016. *'Mammoth discovery? Jurassic Park takes a step closer to reality as Russian scientists find "blood" in woolly mammoth,'* The Independent led with three years prior. Almost three decades on from its release, the film has become shorthand for a certain nervousness surrounding unchecked scientific inquiry.

Yet, alongside its science fiction leanings, *Jurassic Park* is so much more: a creature feature thanks to its state-of-the-art recreation of dinosaurs and explicit references to the likes of *King Kong* (1933); a mad scientist film, the character embodied here by the scheming and hubristic John Hammond; a family drama via its focus on Tim and Lex, children of divorce; an action adventure blockbuster the like of which Spielberg perfected with the Indiana Jones series; and a *Frankenstein*-esque morality tale that teaches mankind a firm lesson for having arrogance enough to believe it can control life and death. Spielberg's deft handling of the story's core sci-fi components allows him to take advantage of its flexibility and pull these other genres into the mix without it feeling awkward or cumbersome.

He prioritises one genre above the others though. Horror joins science fiction as *Jurassic Park*'s key defining genre thanks to its gruesome deaths and suspenseful atmosphere. The film opens with the shocking demise of a Park worker who is killed by a velociraptor, closes with a cat-and-mouse chase between a raptor and the two kids that would not seem out of place in a slasher movie, and hinges on the famous T-Rex attack, during which Spielberg displays a fiendish glee in putting Tim and Lex's lives in danger. As critic Patrick H. Willems notes in his video essay, 'Steven Spielberg and the Horror Inside Blockbusters', the genre is critical to *Jurassic Park*'s make-up:

> 'While most blockbuster set pieces, especially in the past 20 years, are designed to be fun or cool or mildly exciting, Spielberg's goal here is to terrify us. The filmmaking vocabulary he's working with isn't dissimilar to scenes from *Halloween*, *Alien* or *Night of the Living Dead*. Like the most memorable sequences in those movies, this is about things trying to kill people and those people trying desperately to stay alive. (Willems, 2017)

The focus on horror was a point of controversy when the film was released. Concerns were raised about its suitability for family audiences, and even Spielberg confirmed that he would not allow his young children to see it because it was 'too intense' (in Lister, 1993). In the UK, the British Board of Film Classification (BBFC) even went so far as to insist that the poster and other advertisements included a 'rider' offering further explanation of what parents might expect. 'Parents are warned that this film contains sequences which may be particularly disturbing to younger children or children of a sensitive disposition,' the note read (Lister, 1993).

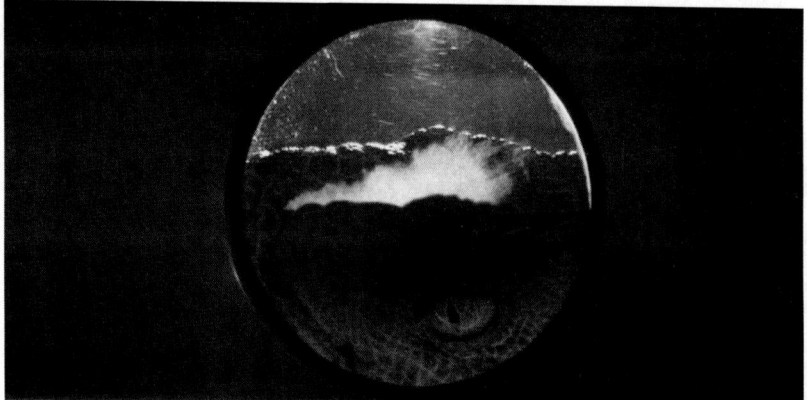

*Figure 2: Through the velociraptors Spielberg indulges his long-held fascination with horror. (© Universal Pictures / Amblin Entertainment)*

With Amblin's animation *The Land Before Time* (1988) and Disney/Jim Henson TV sitcom 'Dinosaurs' (1991-94) firmly establishing dinosaur media within the realm of child-friendly entertainment and Spielberg's name so firmly associated with wholesome family fun, *Jurassic Park*'s horror inflections were a risk, but not an unsurprising one. While Spielberg has never directed a cut-and-dried horror, he has incorporated elements of the genre into a number of his other films: most notably *Indiana Jones and the Temple of Doom*, *Jaws* and his productions of *Poltergeist* (1982), *Gremlins* (1984) and *Arachnophobia* (1990). 'I love this kind of nightmare,' he said while promoting the latter. 'I like to feel my skin crawling under my shirt trying to get up to my jugular vein. I'm diabolical in that sense. I get perverse pleasure in making people sweat in their underwear' (Taylor, 1992: 22).

# CONSTELLATIONS

It is a pleasure that stems back to his youth. Jittery as a child, the young Spielberg was scared by almost everything. 'I was afraid of small spaces, and I was afraid of the tree outside my window,' he told CNN in 2001. 'I had all these phobias... I think many kids have those phobias, but I probably had more than most.' In time, however, he used his imagination to form them into stories in order to gain control. 'There was a crack in the wall by my bed that I stared at all the time, imagining little friendly people living in the crack and coming out to talk to me,' he has said. 'One day while I was staring at the crack it suddenly widened. It opened about five inches and little pieces fell out of it. I screamed a silent scream. I couldn't get anything out. I was frozen... I liked being scared. It was very stimulating.' (Baxter, 1997: 21).

What Spielberg is describing is a form of catharsis, and it is absolutely imperative to the horror genre and Spielberg's use of it in conjunction with science fiction. If, as Pramaggiore and Wallis argue, sci-fi films are about our relationship with science and technology, they explore it by imagining two opposing forces (chaos and control) and crashing them together: we seek control through our technology, but the world pushes back with chaos. Horror does this too, but on a more primal and emotional level, grabbing viewers by '[their] jugular vein' and really making them 'sweat in their underwear'.

We should not like watching horror films, which delight in showing us unpleasant things we would not want to see in real life because they feel uncontrollable. On the cinema screen, however, these sights become more palatable and even enjoyable. In the safety of the theatre, we call the shots: deciding whether or not to see the film, when to look away, when to leave for a conveniently-timed bathroom break. We experience the danger and learn our lessons from it without having to actually live it.

By playing so fast and loose with genre, and by blending science fiction and horror specifically, Spielberg could create with *Jurassic Park* a unique, thrilling, wondrous, terrifying and thought-provoking film that allows him to foreground ideas of chaos and control and explore them intellectually via the sci-fi elements and viscerally through the horror aspects. In doing so, the film is part of his transition from the crowd-pleasing entertainer to the more socially-aware public figure he became.

## READING *JURASSIC PARK*

To explore how he did this, I have chosen to divide this book into three core themes: nature, cinematic reality and immersion, and masculinity. My decision has been driven, in part, by the fact that these concepts were shifting significantly at the start of the 1990s. Advances in science would eventually lead to the famous cloning of Dolly the Sheep in 1996 and a change in humanity's relationship with nature. The massive innovations in special effects technology made the concept of cinematic reality flexible enough for filmmakers to imagine almost anything, put it up on screen and convince us it is real. Meanwhile the 'Hardbody Hero' ethos popularised by the likes of Arnold Schwarzenegger and Sylvester Stallone during the 1980s was fading away in favour of the softer and more sensitive New Man. *Jurassic Park* was born during a period of societal and cultural change, and Spielberg and Crichton drew on it when telling their stories.

More than that, however, my analysis is driven by the context of Spielberg's career. Over the course of five decades, Spielberg has crafted a body of work that is compelling in its diversity, as we have seen, but also its focus on certain key themes. From *Duel*'s (1971) David Mann (Dennis Weaver) battling the harsh American desert to Sophie (Ruby Barnhill) collecting dreams next to a gigantic tree in *The BFG*, nature has always been a vital part of Spielberg's cinema. The same can be said of the concept of perception and the way we view the world around us, which Spielberg has tapped into through the notion of 'the Spielberg Face' amongst other things. Meanwhile, *Jaws* stands as one of American cinema's greatest interrogations of controlling and violent masculinity, a concern Spielberg has maintained throughout his career and specifically focused on in 2017's *The Post*, which explores the way women struggle to find space and success in a patriarchal world.

I will also look at Spielberg's life because he himself believes a director's personal experiences are key to the films they produce. Speaking to Empire magazine in 2018, he explained: 'I think every movie comes from every filmmaker's life, even if it's not on the nose. Every choice a filmmaker makes is informed by the collection of life experiences that led up to the moment of making that choice. So every film is a personal film' (Freer, 2018). He has even remarked on how specific scenes reflect particular episodes from his life. *E.T.* is famously inspired by the divorce of his parents, Leah and Arnold, and *Close Encounters* by his father taking him and his sisters out at night to witness meteor showers.

More recently, he revealed that a scene in *Bridge of Spies* where James Donovan finds his son filling the bathtub with water in preparation for a Soviet attack was something he himself did as a child: 'I wrote that scene,' he told The Hollywood Reporter. 'It's as close to my life as you can get' (Lewis, 2015). Meanwhile, *Lincoln* was inspired by a childhood visit to the Lincoln Memorial: 'It absolutely terrified me. Because it was just so massive. Colossal. And I was so small. When my uncle saw that I was frightened, we left. I turned around and looked at the face of Lincoln and I suddenly wasn't frightened anymore' (in Podrazik, 2012). The memory seems seared into the film, which is bookended by scenes of a silhouetted President looming benignly over the frame.

Judging Spielberg's films without taking into account the personal and professional incidents that have impacted them would be to underestimate them and overlook key elements. As he told Susan Lacy's 2017 documentary *Spielberg*: 'I avoided therapy. Movies are my therapy.'

## Synopsis

Isla Nublar. It is night and the trees are rustling in the jungle. A group of construction workers led by warden Robert Muldoon (Bob Peck) are looking towards the source of the disturbance. A large crate emerges from the trees. It is gently craned into place beside a large concrete paddock. Muldoon and his team regard the crate with caution, arming and aiming their weapons to ensure it is smoothly unloaded. However, disaster strikes when a worker slips and is dragged to his death by the crate's occupant: a velociraptor.

Paleontologists Dr. Alan Grant (Sam Neill) and Dr. Ellie Sattler (Laura Dern) are at a dig in the Badlands of Montana. They are visited by an enigmatic businessman called John Hammond (Richard Attenborough), who tells them about a mysterious project that he needs their expert advice on. Promising them enough money to fund their

# Jurassic Park

endeavours for the next several years, Hammond secures Grant and Sattler's services and they venture to Isla Nublar alongside lawyer Donald Gennaro (Martin Ferraro) and mathematician Dr. Ian Malcolm (Jeff Goldblum), who will also lend his insight to Hammond's venture.

The group arrives at the island and is taken to a clearing where they see a brachiosaur grazing on nearby trees. Hammond has built a theme park filled with living dinosaurs. Eager to show off his process for bringing the creatures back to life, Hammond takes the group to the Park's Visitors Centre, where they see the lab in which the dinosaurs are bred. Following a concerning trip to the raptor pen we saw at the start of the film, the group sit down over dinner to discuss the park's potential successes and failings. Malcolm, Sattler and Grant all express misgivings, while Gennaro is excited by the money they can make.

Much to the child-phobic Grant's chagrin, the group is joined by Hammond's grandchildren Lex and Tim (Ariana Richards and Joseph Mazzello) and they set out on a tour of the park together. However, nothing runs as planned. The dinosaurs do not appear in their enclosures and the group escapes the car to tend to a sick Triceratops. Soon, a storm starts brewing and the group heads back to its touring vehicles, save for Sattler who stays behind with the dinosaur. Meanwhile, in the Park's Control Room, computer technician Dennis Nedry (Wayne Knight) plans to disable the Park's security and shut off its power as part of a plot to steal a collection of dinosaur embryos for Hammond's business rivals.

As a result, the tour cars stop on their way back to the Visitors Centre. Their final location is outside of a tyrannosaurus rex's paddock. The Rex appears and breaks out of its pen. Terrified, Gennaro flees the car he is in with Lex and Tim, leaving the children alone. The Rex's attention is drawn to their car and it attacks them as Grant and Malcolm watch on from the other car in shock. The Rex flips the children's car over, putting them at risk of being crushed. Finally, Grant and Malcolm take action, distracting the beast. Malcolm is injured and Gennaro killed in the chaos, but Grant, Lex and Tim escape into the Park.

Nedry has his own run-in with a dinosaur: a dilophosaur, which blinds and kills him. Sattler is now back at the Control Room and she, Hammond, Muldoon and Nedry's

# CONSTELLATIONS

fellow technician Ray Arnold (Samuel L. Jackson) realise that Nedry is not going to reappear and so the power and security systems cannot be easily restored. With the dinosaurs able to roam wherever they like, drastic action needs to be taken and they reboot the system entirely. To get everything back online, however, someone needs to venture to a maintenance shed. Arnold volunteers and is killed, so Sattler and Muldoon take on the responsibility, but during their efforts Muldoon is trapped and killed by raptors.

Concurrently, Grant, Lex and Tim are making their way through the Park. Grant's earlier reticence around the children has faded and he has now taken on a paternal role for them, promising to stay awake and warn them of incoming dinosaurs while they sleep and ushering them away when the Rex reappears. While Sattler is restoring the power, the trio are attempting to climb a fence that will become electrified when Sattler succeeds. Grant and Lex climb over in time, but fear strikes Tim, who clings on for too long and is electrocuted when the power comes back. Only first aid from Grant saves the boy's life.

Returning to the Visitors' Centre, Grant and Sattler are reunited. Lex and Tim have gone to find something to eat, but are spotted by a pack of raptors and have to flee into a kitchen and hide. The raptors follow and only some quick thinking from the children helps them escape the dinosaurs' clutches. They find Grant and Sattler, but the raptors are relentless, pursuing the group through the Visitors' Centre, until they are finally in the foyer, where the humans are surrounded. All hope seems lost, but out of nowhere the Rex appears and kills the raptors, giving Grant, Sattler, Lex and Tim time to escape.

The quartet is picked up by Hammond and Malcolm and taken to a helicopter to escape the island. Sattler notices Grant's new closeness with Tim and Lex and the two share a smile. Grant looks out of the helicopter's window and notices a flock of birds flying alongside them as they travel at sunset back to civilisation.

# CHAPTER I: ADVENTURES ON EARTH

Before *Jurassic Park*, little respect had been paid to the dinosaurs of cinema's past. Years of cheesy B-movies and cheap serials meant that the T-Rex, stegosaurus and brontosaurus were almost uniformly positioned as hideous beasts to be cowered from or killed – monsters rather than animals. Though these films formed part of his cultural DNA as a child, Spielberg never saw dinosaurs in quite the same way. A resident of the Haddonfield area of New Jersey in his early years, he grew up in a place of huge paleontological significance: the first almost-complete dinosaur skeleton recovered in modern times, the Hadrosaurus foulkii, was found in Haddonfield in 1858 (McBride, 2010: 60). History was not just words written in textbooks for Spielberg, and dinosaurs were not just alive on the movie screen. The very land the boy stood on vibrated with echoes of the prehistoric past.

In one respect, making *Jurassic Park* was a way for Spielberg to reconnect with his childhood: he has spoken of how 'some of my first largest words were triceratops and stegosaurus and that he wanted to make 'a movie for all those dinosaur lovers' (Bouzereau, 2011). But to do this, he knew he had to buck the trends of the past and aim for realism. Speaking on the documentary 'The Making of Jurassic Park', he explained: '[We wanted people to say]: "Gee, this is the first time I've really seen a dinosaur. This isn't *Gorgo*, this isn't *Godzilla*. This is a real movie that I think is really happening as I'm watching it"' (Schultz, 1995). In conversation with Jody Duncan and Don Shay, he went even further: 'I wanted my dinosaurs to be animals. I wouldn't even let anyone call them monsters or creatures.' (Shay and Duncan, 1993: 15-16)

Such was Spielberg's attention to detail that he even insisted on the dinosaurs having clear and distinct personalities, which he worked out with Michael Crichton in the early days of the film's development. Crichton explained:

> [Spielberg] went through every character in the story, outlining their physical appearances, their motivations, their hopes and fears, their quirks and foibles. Ideas about dialogue, gestures, and costuming tumbled out. Speaking very rapidly, he went on like this for an hour. At last he turned to the dinosaurs, but again, he spoke of them as characters. The strength and limitations of the tyrannosaur. The

quick menace of the velociraptors. The sick triceratops... Finally, I could stand it no longer. 'Steven', I said, 'how are you going to do this?' He shrugged, and made a little dismissing gesture with his hand. Not important. Not what we need to talk about... I said, 'But these effects-'. 'Effects', he said, 'are only as good as the audience's feeling for the characters.' (in McBride, 2010: 421)

Through decision-making such as this, Spielberg not only ensured that *Jurassic Park* reconsidered the way dinosaurs were presented on the big screen, but also set its sight on something bigger: humanity's relationship with nature as a whole. It is a key recurring theme in Spielberg's cinema and one he evolves here as he questions how much humanity can benefit from the natural world before we start to corrupt and exploit it. To understand the way he does this, this chapter will analyse Spielberg's approach to nature, his depiction of suburbia, and the way he alienates humanity in *Jurassic Park*.

## THE GREEN WORLD

Following their time in New Jersey, Spielberg and his family moved to Arcadia in Phoenix, Arizona. Sharing its name with the utopian vision of rural harmony, Arcadia was low on entertainment options ('We had nothing! Except, probably, the worst television you've ever seen,' Spielberg has said (in Crawley, 1983: 13)), but high on natural wonder. The striking sight of Camelback Mountain looms as large over the landscape as Devil's Tower does Wyoming, and elsewhere natural beauty is plentiful, thanks in part to remnants of the citrus groves it is built on. This was particularly tangible for Spielberg; the family garden boasted beautiful orange trees, and he delighted in finding mischievous ways to use them. 'Steven loved to take the rotten ones that had fallen off and practice his pitching – by making us his human targets,' his sister Sue told Anna Goldenberg. 'A typical fun summer activity – we'd run from tree to tree while he'd try to hit us with the oranges!' (Goldenberg, 2015)

It was not just childish games that occupied the young Spielberg's mind in Arcadia; clear blue skies and beautiful dark nights meant that grander things were at play too.

The atmosphere was clear there. We had a lot of starry nights. I remember when my father woke me up one night and took me to a hillside at about 3am. He spread out a blanket and we sat there and watched a fabulous meteor shower. It was... extraordinary! I wanted to know what put those points of light up there. (in Crawley, 1983: 9)

This was not a one-off occasion. If there was a meteor shower in Arcadia and the weather was good enough to offer a clear view, Arnold would get his children out of bed and journey outside to observe the wonder (Goldenberg, 2015). So impactful were these incidents that Spielberg has paid tribute to them by including a shooting star in a handful of his films – including *Jaws*, *Indiana Jones and the Temple of Doom* and *Catch Me If You Can* – but the influence of Arcadia's natural beauty can be seen in almost all of his movies, and especially his early ones, where characters are repeatedly forced out of their domestic comfort zone and into their natural surroundings.

*Duel*'s David Mann, for example, is driven into the wilds of the American desert; Martin Brody is pushed onto the oceans of Amity; Roy Neary develops an obsession with Devil's Tower; Indiana Jones battles evil against the vastness of deserts and jungles, and E.T. – the purest character Spielberg has ever put on screen – is entirely associated with nature: he is an alien botanist who travels from planet to planet to observe and catalogue their plant life. Nature is an ever-present for Spielberg, and as Michael Koresky notes in an analysis of *Always* (1989) for the online journal Reverse Shot (2012), Spielberg's world 'is a green world'.

Koresky's essay is a significant influence on this chapter, and it goes on to outline how Spielberg uses nature to explore the divine: a 'triangular relationship between God, man and nature'. My reading, however, is more secular. Spielberg's Green World is indeed a wondrous one, but it is more about people's connection with each other and themselves than a divine presence. Nature offers itself up as a canvas for humanity to paint its emotions on and by engaging with it respectfully we can find our better instincts (connection, compassion, empathy) reflected in it and consequently form a harmonious relationship with it. However, the exact opposite also exists within Spielberg's films: the man-made world, or 'The Grey World' as it could be termed, relating as it does to the concrete buildings and tarmacked roads of the city. This is a place of disconnect, selfishness and apathy, a corrupt place where all we see is our own base instincts.

Speaking with Laurent Bouzereau in an interview (2000) for a home video release of *Lawrence of Arabia* (1962), Spielberg offered the following telling insight:

> I was raised in the desert, so I had an affinity for Lawrence's love of the desert. I understood [Lawrence's] obsession with how clean the desert was. That's what I always thought: that the desert was cleaner than the city and the neighbourhoods. Nature just swept all the debris out of the desert and kept it pristine every moment. It was that moment of Lawrence and nature at one with each other that I really could relate to.

It is difficult to believe that Spielberg would take such a dim view of the city and its surrounding suburbs, that he would see them as somehow unclean and corrupt. We tend to think of him as one of the great devotees of urban America, but he himself has admitted his reticence to make 'a city film' (Ebert and Siskel, 1991: 71) and his depiction of suburbia is more complex than public and critical perception suggests. Displaying both a deep love for the comfort that suburban togetherness provides and a significant resentment of the confines it imposes, Spielberg rages against and embraces it in many of his most famous films. As Joseph McBride writes: 'Spielberg does not entirely believe in [suburbia], share its values, or depict it in quite such glowing terms [as many people think] on screen... the suburbia to which his upwardly mobile parents escaped in the early 1950s becomes a place of entrapment from which his dissatisfied middle-class characters yearn to escape' (McBride, 2010: 49).

His distrust of this Grey World began with his very first film. *Duel* primarily takes place in the desert, but suburbia lines its edges. Mann is a frustrated husband and office drone. He is only on the road because he has to travel to a business meeting and seems trapped in a corporate world he does not want to be a part of and struggles to compete in. He is too apathetic to do anything about it though, and his challenge is to shake off the complacency it has imposed on him. Speaking in a 1978 interview with Time Out magazine, Spielberg outlined the kind of numb suburbanite Mann represents:

It begins on a Sunday: you take your car to be washed. You have to drive it but it's only a block away. And, as the car's being washed, you go next door with the kids and buy them ice-cream at the Dairy Queen and then you have lunch at the plastic McDonald's with seven zillion hamburgers sold. And then you go off to the games room and you play the quarter games: Tank and the Pong and Flim-Flam. And by that time you go back and your car's all dry and ready to go and you get into the car and you drive to the Magic Mountain plastic amusement park and you spend the day there eating junk food.

Afterwards, you drive home, stopping at all the red lights, and the wife is waiting with dinner on. And you have instant potatoes and eggs without cholesterol because they're artificial – and you sit down and turn on the television set, which has become the reality as opposed to the fantasy this man has lived with that entire day. And you watch the primetime, which is pabulum and nothing more than watching a night-light. And you see the news at the end of that, which you don't want to listen to because it doesn't conform to the reality you've just been through primetime with. And at the end of all that you go to sleep and you dream about making enough money to support weekend America (Pirie, 1978).

We also see this frustration in *Jaws* and *War of the Worlds*, which depict the descent of seemingly passive neighbourhoods into mobs driven by panic and self-preservation, and in *E.T.* and *Close Encounters*, which follow *Duel*'s lead by portraying suburbia as bland and suffocating. Elliott's mother Mary struggles to cope with her children in the claustrophobia of her small home, while Roy's anger with his kids boils over so much that he refuses to help them with their homework and even passive-aggressively threatens them. *Close Encounters* is, as Frederick Wasser notes, 'a portrait of a man frustrated by the limited imagination of those around him, in both his family and his neighbourhood' (Wasser, 2010: 82). Meanwhile, Clélia Cohen notes that 'American symbols' litter the film ('Shell and McDonald's logos, TV soaps and Budweiser ads, "Coca-Cola" labelled trucks serving as a cover for the army's planned masquerade') and calls Neary 'a man at odds with America' (Cohen, 2010: 29)

In many cases, it is only by engaging with The Green World that these Grey World characters can become at one with themselves, others and the world around them.

## CONSTELLATIONS

However, their journeys from one place to the other are not always benign; as Koresky notes 'Spielberg's landscapes can turn malevolent when the sun goes down'. So Spielberg uses two distinct character arcs to track these journeys; they can be dubbed the Trial by Nature and the Symbiosis with Nature. Both have ultimately positive effects, forcing characters into the revelatory landscape of The Green World, but deliver them in very different ways. In a Trial by Nature, a character is pitted against the elements and forced to prove his or her strength. In a Symbiosis with Nature, there is no such friction: nature arrives as a pure force to complement and enhance a character's life.

The first two Indiana Jones films illuminate the difference. In *Raiders of the Lost Ark*, Indy is assisted by nature. He finds the Well of Souls by harnessing the power of the sun through the Staff of Ra, and later digs towards it against a backdrop of brilliant orange sunlight. This is an instance of Symbiosis with Nature because there is a sense of total harmony between Indy and the natural world that helps transform him into a better, more humble person. *E.T.* and *The BFG* follow a similar path and can also be considered examples of Spielberg's Symbiosis with Nature motif.

*Indiana Jones and the Temple of Doom*, on the other hand, offers an example of a Trial by Nature. Here, Indy ventures into the bowels of the earth in pursuit of 'fortune and glory' and as he does so nature seems to resist. With Pankot Palace and the eponymous temple drawing nearer, Spielberg and cinematographer Douglas Slocombe bathe the film in blood reds and dark tones that speak more of hell than the wonder of Earth. The film's finale has Indy and the villainous Mola Ram (Amrish Puri) battling on a crumbling rope bridge over a ravine. It is nature's final reckoning and only once Mola Ram has been eaten alive by crocodiles and Indy has restored the Sankara Stones to their rightful place can nature truly win and harmony be restored. *Duel*, *Jaws* and *Empire of the Sun* are other examples of Trial by Nature.

Spielberg also blends Trial and Symbiosis, notably in *War Horse* (2011), which shows how the brutality of conflict can poison the purity of nature (symbolised by the horse Joey), and during the kidnapping scene from *Close Encounters*. Dominated by a multitude of red, orange, blue and purple light, this moment contains what Spielberg told Gene Siskel and Roger Ebert is his 'master image': the shot of Barry Guiler (Carey

# Jurassic Park

Guffey) opening the door to the visitors and standing, totally serene, in the door frame surrounded by glowing orange (Siskel and Ebert, 1990). Before this, Spielberg fills the scene with examples of natural wonder. The clouds part and the atmosphere itself seems to burn as the tension builds and the alien ships emerge. When the visitors have finally claimed Barry following their terrifying assault, they return to the sky, disappearing into the clouds as if they didn't come from space at all, but nature itself. The scene closes on an extreme wide shot that captures the Guiler house, the landscape and the sky together in a single image. Barry's helpless mother Jillian (Melinda Dillon) is a dot against the awe-inspiring wonder of nature as she screams for her son's safe return.

A moment that blends wonder and fear, this is a Trial by Nature for Jillian, who cannot conceive of this as anything other than a horrifying experience, but Symbiosis with Nature for Barry, who recognises the visitors as the wondrous beings they are. Only at the end of the film, when the visitors return – again from the clouds and above the stunning backdrop of Devil's Tower – will Jillian see the truth and accept them as her son accepts them.

## DINOSAURS RULE THE EARTH

*Jurassic Park* fits the *Close Encounters* mould, being both Trial and Symbiosis, but it alters the concept in one key way: here the binary is not entirely focused on human characters. Breaking the relationship he had previously built, Spielberg shows how Grey World engagement with The Green World has become exploitation. As a result, *Jurassic Park* envisions humanity and nature as two separate entities running in parallel: together, but separate. To a degree, The Green World remains a canvas for Grey World protagonists to project onto and grow through, but it has more autonomy, a sense of agency. It is not just a location – a desert, an ocean, a forest – but living, breathing dinosaurs, who of course Spielberg was so determined to flesh out as real characters the audience could understand and relate to.

In this sense, The Green World becomes so autonomous that it even enjoys Symbiosis with itself while the human characters endure the Trial. This means that while Grant and the kids are dragged through the mud in their attempts to survive the Park, the dinosaurs adapt and thrive, with the T-Rex in particular reclaiming its dominion over Isla Nublar during the finale, with a banner reading WHEN DINOSAURS RULED THE EARTH triumphantly cascading to the ground around it, in case we miss the symbolism. It is Trial and Symbiosis, but used as a way to underline the split between Green and Grey Worlds, humanity and nature, rather than the bond between them.

This split is caused by humanity's hubris and its attempts to enforce the greed of The Grey World onto The Green World. By creating Jurassic Park, Hammond has done more than just try to set up a fun weekend getaway destination. This is an attack, an attempt to relocate a 'Magic Mountain plastic amusement park' (Pirie, 1978) to an untouched tropical paradise and, in the words of Ian Malcolm, patent that paradise, package it, slap it on a plastic lunchbox and sell it. With the covenant between Green and Grey Worlds severed, harmony cannot be easily restored. Instead there is respect, a peace treaty, which is symbolised through a complex final shot that I will return to later in this chapter.

The tension between the Green and Grey Worlds was a key part of the film's make-up from the very start. As Malia Scotch Marmo, who wrote the first draft of the screenplay, told Don Shay and Jody Duncan:

*Figure 3: The human world invades the natural world in the opening scene of Jurassic Park. (© Universal Pictures / Amblin Entertainment)*

> I wanted to show the fatal flaw in trying to control nature. And I did that by juxtaposing a lot of jungle imagery with the pristine control room – things like having one wall of the visitor centre uncompleted so that greenery is pushing in and vines are swinging down. Small things like windows being opened and vegetation bursting inside and little lizards that run across the sidewalk. The idea was that nature was always in the way, always pushing hard against the intrusion. (Shay and Duncan, 1993: 42)

Spielberg emphasises the extent of this control and the alienating effect it has on humanity from the outset through a trilogy of connected scenes. These scenes are all laced with direct or suggested violence towards nature and reverse Hammond's de-extinction process by showing us, first, a live dinosaur, then the DNA required to create it and finally the fossils that represent the real dinosaur. By doing so, Spielberg is undermining The Grey World, and Hammond's attempts at control before the character has even appeared on screen. The scenes are:

(1) The arrival of a velociraptor into its pen and the death of a Park worker;

(2) The arrival of Gennaro at the South American amber mine and his introduction to digger Juanito (Miguel Sandoval);

(3) The excavation of a fossil by Grant, Sattler and their team of diggers in the Badlands of Montana.

In the opening scene, we are given our first glimpse of the chaos the Park will unleash. Muldoon and his workers attempt to usher the raptor into its pen, only for things to go disastrously wrong when one of the workers gets dragged inside and killed. It is The Green World striking its first blow against The Grey, the first indication that man will experience a Trial by Nature and nature itself a Symbiosis.

Spielberg uses nature to underline a sense of dread from the outset by opening the film with ambient jungle noises that play over the Universal logo. This lasts for 27 seconds before John Williams' foreboding music thuds into life and the credits appear. It is almost as if the film itself is intruding into the natural world.

Darkness that reflects the blackness of the jungle at night fills the screen for another 25 seconds, before we finally fade into the film proper. Nature again dominates as tree branches fill the screen, the music replaced by the sound of wood crashing and leaves rustling. A group of Park workers look up at the sight, before Spielberg pushes in on Muldoon, gun at the ready, dressed in the hunter gear that will be his costume throughout. Williams' music – a low electronic pounding like the beating of a heart – starts up once more.

In a film high on tension, this is one of *Jurassic Park*'s most nerve-shredding scenes. But the dangerous element is not the just raptor; indeed, aside from a fleeting glimpse of an eye and the sound of snarling, we do not see the dinosaur at all during the scene. Instead, the tension is generated by the humans, with Spielberg focusing primarily on their actions and how they are intruding on The Green World.

As the crate is pushed from the trees and lowered into place, Spielberg captures its descent with a low-angle shot, while the whirring of the crane dominates the soundtrack. The crate passes over the camera, making the audience feel part of the scene and under threat, not from the raptor, but the crane: one false move, and it falls on top of us. Its journey is captured in a 26-second long shot that moves from jungle to landing position. The hard, grey angles of the landing position and blinding lights that surround it dominate the frame as Spielberg blots out the soft greens, browns and blacks of the jungle. In a single shot, The Green World has lost out and The Grey World has taken over.

The first clue Spielberg gives as to the contents of the crate comes from a point of view shot when the raptor peers through a gap in the box at Muldoon and his men and snorting can be heard on the soundtrack. Next, he cuts to the outside of the crate again as more men surround it, like an invading army, ready to push it into place. 'I want tasers on full charge,' says Muldoon leaving us under no illusion as to where the power lies. A brief cut back to the inside of the crate and a squeal from the raptor pushes the power back a little but the men persist.

Muldoon orders his team to carry on performing their tasks, and Spielberg frames him in the centre of most of the shots he is in: a sergeant in full control. The grey and blue tones of the metallic crate continue to inform the colour and lighting of each shot, furthering the men's belief that their Grey World has control over The Green World. However, when the crate is opened, control is lost: the raptor charges, the man opening the crate falls and his fate is sealed. Disorder reigns and Muldoon and the raptor lock eyes, Spielberg showing us close-ups of both. Man and nature, the Grey and the Green, are bound in chaos.

Even with all their guns and technology – all the strength of The Grey World – at their disposal, the workers are powerless to stop the might of the raptor. Muldoon's cries of 'Shoot her! Shoot her!' as the dinosaur claims its victim represent a last bid to assert man's power over nature; an attempt emphasised by Spielberg's extreme close up of Muldoon's mouth. But it is to no avail. The unfortunate worker slips from Muldoon's grasp and into the clutches of the raptor. The Grey World has been thwarted in this attempt to assert control, but that will not stop it.

Fading from the deceased worker's hand grasping for survival to water rippling as Gennaro is ferried across it to land, Spielberg moves into the second scene in this sequence by affirming man's persistence in disrupting nature. Dressed in an expensive grey suit and clutching an equally luxurious briefcase, Gennaro is the embodiment of The Grey World and utterly at odds with his surroundings, which are dominated by browns and greens and populated by miners who are dirtied by the earth they are digging up. He represents selfishness and greed, and talks of how the insurance companies and investors involved in the creation of the Park are anxious after the events of the previous scene. The basic decency required to acknowledge the death of a man as anything other than a threat to business seems to elude Gennaro.

Moving into the mine, Gennaro watches Juanito examine a rock of amber, but rather than standing in awe at nature's majesty, he continues to talk business, enquiring about Alan Grant and asking why Juanito thinks he will refuse to visit the island and sign-off on its safety. 'Grant is like me,' Juanito says. 'He's a digger.' It is a state of mind Gennaro will never understand. The scene ends with a set-up Spielberg has used many times before as he zooms in on the rock while Juanito, Gennaro and a group of miners gather around it: the wonder of nature magnified for the audience. Backlighting from the miners' lamps makes the orange of the amber glow brighter, underlining its majesty, but the context of the scene, and Williams' dark and unsettling music, bode ill. Humanity has extracted more than a rock with a dead insect inside; we have taken the very essence of life from the earth, and in doing so, created a rift in our relationship with The Green World that we will struggle to heal.

It is here that Spielberg cuts to the third and final scene in the sequence, which finds Grant and Sattler excavating dinosaur bones. Of the three scenes, this condemns humanity and The Grey World the least, but it still shares something in common with its predecessors – it positions the technology of The Grey World as an invasive force. It begins with a series of close-ups of bones being excavated, Spielberg eventually revealing the full, unearthed skeleton as mysterious Williams music plays on the soundtrack. This is nature at its purest and while Muldoon and Gennaro are positioned as aggressive invaders in their scenes, Grant and Sattler are discoverers, carefully and sensitively engaging with nature at its source.

However, as the scene develops, we are shown a radar machine that allows the group to identify buried fossils without having to dig, an idea that is itself an indication of The Grey World's refusal to engage directly with The Green World. To perform its function, the machine invasively shoots a large metal pellet into the ground. When the action takes place, it is fired with the force of a shotgun in a moment that brings an abrupt end to Williams' score and momentarily pauses the film into a few seconds of quiet, during which the only sound is the dust disturbed by the penetration settling again. It is another example of The Grey World encroaching into The Green, but The Green World fires back. The radar image the computer captures is distorted, suggesting that even here, in these relatively primitive attempts at technology-enhanced paleontology, humanity's attempts to gain control over nature are flawed.

It is fitting, then, that this sequence of scenes concludes with the ultimate source of humanity's hubris arriving. Hammond lands on the site in his helicopter, blowing the earth cleared from the fossil back over it. The debris is literally being swept back into the desert, the embodiment of The Grey World is staking his claim to The Green World.

## DEBUG THE SYSTEM

As the film progresses, The Grey World exerts an even greater hold, particularly through technology, and Spielberg uses colour and composition to further its alienating effects when Hammond, Gennaro, Grant, Sattler and Malcolm arrive at Isla Nublar. Through a series of wide shots designed to convey the power of the natural world and relative redundancy of humanity's own inflated sense of power, Spielberg depicts the helicopter the group is travelling in as a tiny dot against the vast expanse of the ocean, and then the island itself, which emerges into view just as Williams' rousing main theme begins. It is a triumphant moment, but the music and camerawork do not celebrate the park or Hammond's creation of it, because we have not actually seen it yet. Instead, the island in all its untampered majesty is being celebrated. This is The Green World at its purest.

As we move closer to the first signs of the park, and The Grey World it represents, the tone begins to shift. The silver and blue helicopter descends (turbulence causing the vehicle to shake, almost as a final warning to its occupants to turn back), and as it does, Spielberg tracks its path against the backdrop of a cascading waterfall. This builds a sense of disconnect: the natural descent of the water is juxtaposed with the unnatural descent of the artificial machine. Hammond and company are invaders and Spielberg is subtly sounding the alarm.

More vehicles (jeeps) appear once the helicopter has landed and colour is again used to promote disharmony: the cars are painted in a block primary colour that lacks nuance and subtlety (red) and a plain, dull grey. (The film's most prominent vehicles – the touring cars that appear later – follow a similar pattern. Here the primary colours are green, red and yellow.) The jeeps reverse into a shot that uses the waterfall as background, intrusively blocking our view of it, and as the scene progresses, they move through an electrified fence, which slams shut, imprisoning the hills, waterfall and palm trees. Nature has been neutered in Jurassic Park and replaced with a man-made world ruled not by natural law, but computers, electrified fences and lines of code.

# CONSTELLATIONS

*Figure 4: Spielberg frames the natural beauty of Isla Nublar behind electrified fences in the island's introduction. (© Universal Pictures / Amblin Entertainment)*

The character identified with this web of technology is the only outright villain of *Jurassic Park*: Dennis Nedry. Though Hammond, Grant, Gennaro and Muldoon all have negative elements to their personalities, none damage The Green World as badly, represent The Grey World as firmly or deserve their various fates as much as this cruel, lazy and greedy man does. We first meet him during a covert meeting with Lewis Dodgson (Cameron Thor), a corporate spy who works for a rival of Hammond's InGen. The meeting takes place at a small restaurant in San Jose, Costa Rica. The surrounding area is a little run-down, but the restaurant itself is comparatively tidy and appealing – a place for tourists to dine. Dressed in inconspicuous clothing and wearing sunglasses and a Panama Hat to hide his face, Dodgson's apparel is appropriate to his nefarious purpose, but Nedry is oblivious, or at least uncaring. He is wearing an ostentatiously colourful Hawaiian shirt and calls Dodgson over to his table, mocking him when he complains about Nedry's use of his real name. 'Dodgson! Dodgson! We've got Dodgson here,' he says, shouting and pointing. 'See, nobody cares.'

Both men are pathetic creatures, but Nedry is the more pathetic. Morbidly obese already, he is seen scarfing down food when Dodgson arrives and has more lined up on his plate. It is an awkward portrayal by Spielberg. He seems to be drawing a parallel between Nedry's greed for money and his greed for food, but comes

## Jurassic Park

close to fat-shaming the character. Nedry immediately gets down to business and giggles with glee after being given part of his payment for stealing Jurassic Park's dinosaur embryos ($750,000 with another $50,000 for each viable embryo arriving upon completion of the job). He is like a child tearing its way through the Magic Mountain plastic amusement park Spielberg mentioned in relation to *Duel*. He is the embodiment of everything The Grey World represents and The Green World rejects: selfishness, greed and indifference towards the people his plan will hurt.

His greedy delight continues when Dodgson reveals a fake shaving cream canister that can hold the stolen vials and get them off the island without detection. Nedry releases a little foam onto his hand to ensure it works like any regular canister would, and places the unwanted foam on a slice of nearby pie that will be carted off and served to some unsuspecting customer: a juvenile prank played by a childish man. The scene concludes with the bill arriving and Nedry warning Dodgson not to 'get cheap' because 'that was Hammond's mistake'. Even with $750,000 in front of him, Nedry still wants more.

For most of his scenes, Nedry is in Jurassic Park's nerve centre – the Control Room – alongside Hammond, Muldoon and Arnold. Each of these men have a certain level of power, but Nedry appears to have the most; indeed he seems to possess mastery over life and death itself. 'Dennis,' Hammond says when told of the Park's technical malfunctions, 'our lives are in your hands and you have butterfingers!?' Though the glitches are frustrating for Hammond, his criticisms overlook the incredible feat Nedry has achieved – and the terrible power it has given him and everyone around him. 'You can run this whole Park from this room with minimal staff for up to three days,' he explains. 'You think that kinda automation is easy?' So complete is the power Nedry has attained that he does not even need to be around to wield it. Like the radar excavation machine, it is a simple case of flipping a switch, sitting back and taking control. It is The Grey World at the peak of its arrogant, technology-enhanced power.

Just as they did in the landing sequence, Spielberg's direction and Rick Carter's production design build a sense of disconnect here by alienating man from the natural world. There is no colour in the Control Room, just blacks, whites, greys and the flashing red of LEDs. Machinery dominates, monitors pile one on top of the other and wires are strewn everywhere, like nightmarish technological versions of vines stretching through a jungle: The Grey World replicating The Green World. Against this backdrop, Nedry sits among piles of empty Coca-Cola cans and discarded chocolate bar wrappers, another reference to his (and The Grey World's) untamed greed. A photo of atomic bomb scientist Robert Oppenheimer adorns one of his monitors, and a drawing of a mushroom cloud is stuck to it. 'Now I am become Death, the destroyer of worlds,' Oppenheimer famously said, quoting Hindu scripture. But Oppenheimer did it with a bomb, Nedry does it with a mouse and a keyboard. On different levels, both are harbingers of death, destroyers of nature through science and technology.

Nedry's punishment is doled out when he is killed by the dilophosaur in a moment that is played as nature's revenge. To beat an oncoming storm, Nedry has to hurry to the boat that will take him (and his stolen embryos) off the island. With the rain pouring down hard on his jeep's windscreen and condensation fogging up his glasses, visibility is low and he crashes the vehicle before encountering the dilophosaur. Described as a 'beautiful but deadly' creature, the dinosaur bears little in common with its real-life counterpart: there is no evidence to suggest that it spat paralysing venom or had a colourful frill around its neck. However, Spielberg uses this bit of creative licence not just to remind us of how uncontrollably brutal nature is, but how wondrous it is too. Even as it claims its victim in what is the film's most violent death scene, nature is still beautiful.

Maintaining his use of colour to represent the split between man and nature, Spielberg has Nedry arrive into the scene wearing a bright yellow anorak that automatically distances him from the dark greens, muddy browns and midnight blacks of the jungle. If the San Jose restaurant scene was the 'Magic Mountain plastic amusement park' version of nature that Nedry feels comfortable in, this is the real thing. Of course, he fails to acclimatise, slipping over rocks as he tries to work out how to unstick his jeep from the mud.

A wide shot that tracks Nedry across the jungle and dwarfs him against enormous plants and tree trunks underlines just how out of place he is. This is only cemented

# Jurassic Park

*Figure 5: Spielberg uses colour to highlight how Nedry struggles to fit in amongst nature. (© Universal Pictures / Amblin Entertainment)*

when the dilophosaur appears and, as he did in the scene with Dodgson, Nedry approaches the situation in all the wrong ways, calling the creature a 'nice boy' and a 'nice dinosaur' and trying to distract it by throwing a stick, as one would with a dog. 'Play fetch? Play fetch? Look! Stick, stupid! Fetch the stick!...' he says, underlining his contempt for nature before re-affirming his faith in machinery. 'Ah, no wonder you're extinct. I'm gonna run you over when I come back down.'

Nedry is so unaware of the peril he is in because he has so utterly disassociated himself from nature. He simply cannot think of nature as something that is not domesticated and therefore controlled. So when that nature pushes back, it does so through more than just a death. Gennaro is devoured, Muldoon seized upon and Arnold killed off-screen. These are quick, merciful deaths that Spielberg does not linger over. Nedry, however, is tortured, the dilophosaur toying with him by spitting venom that hits him like splats of mud. The first gob misses his face by inches, but the second smacks him square in the eyes, blinding him. He scrambles his way into the jeep, but the dilophosaur is already there, ready to devour its prey. The embodiment of the greed and selfishness of The Grey World dies trapped in a machine and at the mercy of The Green World.

## CONSTELLATIONS

Wrapping the Nedry storyline up, Spielberg moves his camera from the jeep to the ground, where the lost canister now sits. With rain creating a miniature landslide, the canister is buried by mounds of thick mud, never to be recovered. The Green World has shifted the balance of power against The Grey World, not only destroying the human embodiment of its enslavement, but also returning the embryos to the earth from where they came. From here on in, humanity's Trial will only get worse as the dinosaurs break free and make Isla Nublar their own. It is a Symbiosis with Nature that will give them the autonomy that Hammond and the Park took away.

### LIFE FINDS A WAY

The theme park descends into chaos at this point, but Spielberg is careful not to overplay the horror. The film becomes a steady blend of terror and wonder, Trial and Symbiosis as The Green World reclaims control. For example, shortly after the T-Rex attack, the film's pace slows when Grant, Lex and Tim take refuge in the treetops and encounter a herd of brachiosaurs, whom they pet. Another encounter finds this tonal shift reversed as they admire a flock of sprinting Gallimimuses in a beautiful sequence dominated by the lush green mountains of Isla Nublar. Spielberg spikes the moment with horror – the T-Rex emerging to attack the smaller dinosaurs – but even here there is a sense of respect ('Look at all the blood,' says an awestruck Tim). A natural ecosystem is beginning to emerge and move beyond the control humanity tried to impose.

Only the raptors are denied a sense of majesty, and that's for a good reason. Positioned as the cunning villains of Jurassic Park's animal life, they are our heroes' tormentors, the physical form that humanity's Trial is delivered through. It is telling that they strike primarily around the areas of control – the Visitors' Centre and Control Room – and the people they kill and/or attack are the ones who are trying to restore control: Arnold, Muldoon and eventually Sattler, Grant and the kids. There is very little Symbiosis here, very few moments where we are asked to admire the raptors. These moments are played as pure terror because they need to be. The humans are still clinging to the concept that they can maintain control; their Trial is not yet complete.

# Jurassic Park

It is a Trial that ends in the Visitors' Centre itself. By this point, Grant, Tim and Lex have been defeated by the Park. Caked in mud and covered with cuts and bruises, the trio take shelter in the Visitors' Centre. A pack of raptors is there too and they stalk Tim and Lex in the kitchen. Here, Spielberg employs gallows humour: we have sunk so low in the pecking order that we are now the food. Using low-angle shots, claustrophobic compositions, and the kitchen counters to create a dividing line between the raptors and the kids, Spielberg further establishes the shifting power dynamic. The raptors have mastered Jurassic Park in a way Hammond never could; The Green World has laid claim to The Grey World in a way The Grey could never lay claim to The Green.

This finale, which brings everything to a head, is a marked change from the climaxes of typical Hollywood blockbusters. While most use their final acts to establish a sense of triumph, here Spielberg builds a sense of futility. The kids escape the kitchen and meet up again with Grant and Sattler, but find themselves penned into the Control Room by the raptors, struggling to regain control over the locking system. Lex hacks the database, restoring the security and the control it represents, but the raptors are again relentless, crashing through windows to enter the room and forcing their prey into the air vents above. There is no way for the humans to escape the raptors' grasp and no victory to be found. When one of the raptors cranes its head to work out where Grant, Sattler and the kids are hiding, Spielberg projects genetic code onto its body in one of the film's most striking and famous shots. It is a reminder of where the creature has come from and just how little power we can wield over what was once 'our property'.

Having been forced into the main plaza via the decorative skeletons that hang from the ceiling, the action concludes just when the raptors are ready to pounce. Before they can do so, the T-Rex emerges out of nowhere, stomping into the Visitors' Centre, devouring the raptors and giving Grant, Sattler and the kids sufficient time to escape. The scene was a late addition to the script and a significant diversion from what was originally written. As first planned, the Rex did not return; instead the raptors were to scale the bones, but perish when Grant mans a platform crane, forcing them into the jaws of a T-Rex skeleton and crushing them. It is a neat ending, but one that does not quite fit with the rest of the film. By having Grant kill the raptors and use a machine to do so, humanity re-establishes order: The Grey World beats The Green World. The film's very point is undercut.

With ILM's early CGI special effects work impressing so much, Spielberg changed this approach to give the audience a final glimpse of the T-Rex that he knew would be the film's star, but also to push his core theme. 'When I saw how wonderful and commanding the T-Rex was, I began to feel that the audience would be disappointed if she didn't make a return visit,' he explained. 'Also, it seemed fitting to me, since this movie is really about nature succeeding and man failing, that it is the T-Rex that saves the day' (Shay and Duncan, 1993: 118)

Indeed, when the T-Rex appears, it is only doing what comes naturally: hunting those lower than itself on the food chain. As it does so, Spielberg leaves us under no doubt as to the morality of the moment, giving the Rex an adoring hero shot where it roars triumphantly as the WHEN DINOSAURS RULED THE EARTH banner falls to the ground. The animals of Jurassic Park may be artificial, but they are still animals and by having them create an ecosystem of their own, rather than simply killing them off (or indeed bombing them, as Crichton does in the novel), Spielberg allows nature to restore balance, break free of the interference of man, and snap the food chain back into a natural order, rather than a man-made one.

*Figure 6: The final shot of* Jurassic Park *underlines the relationship Spielberg forges between humanity and nature. (© Universal Pictures / Amblin Entertainment)*

The film's closing scene serves as a complex coda that feeds into this point, as a flock of birds flies alongside the helicopter into a brilliant yellow sunset. The union between humanity and nature that Spielberg traditionally creates at the end of many of his films has not been entirely restored, and nor can it be at this stage. Our abuse of nature was too total, too destructive. But a new harmony has been created in its place. Humanity and nature, The Grey World and The Green World, have entered into a treaty based on respect. Nature is not just a canvas for humanity, but a painting in its own right. By acknowledging that, and not manipulating it, The Grey World and The Green World can live in parallel, together but separate, like the birds and the helicopter. Life, to borrow a phrase, can find a way.

# CHAPTER 2: LIFE THROUGH A LENS

When is a real dinosaur not a real dinosaur? It sounds like one of the jokes Tim tells Alan Grant in the treetops high above Jurassic Park, but it is a key question when exploring the film's themes and ideas. The creatures that John Hammond engineers on Isla Nublar are not actually real dinosaurs. They look like real dinosaurs. They sound like real dinosaurs. They hunt and kill like real dinosaurs. And Hammond certainly does all he can to assert that they are real dinosaurs, boasting over how he 'spared no expense' in creating them. But the fact remains that they are not. Instead, they are representations, beasts built from real dinosaurs' recovered DNA that has then been merged with other bits of genetic code from other animals to create something new: reflections of real dinosaurs, but not real dinosaurs in themselves.

How could they be real? Even if we accept a clone as real, the dinosaurs that Hammond's creatures are based on are long gone, their bones buried by the sands of time, fossilised, dug up by paleontologists and re-assembled into other representations of real dinosaurs. Hammond has made copies of an original that cannot be referenced in full. Our knowledge of dinosaurs is limited, and when our impression of a real dinosaur has been founded upon a representation (through film, artistic impression or fossil recreation), what do we base our acceptance of the copy on? How do we tell reality from representation, fact from fantasy? What, in other words, is real?

In his novel, Michael Crichton repeatedly returns to this question. Characters discuss the reality of the dinosaurs and whether reality even has a place in the confines of theme parks, which by their very nature are built to distract from reality, rather than reproduce it. Take the following exchange between Hammond and his lead scientist Dr. Henry Wu, in which the latter tries to tell his boss that Jurassic Park is not real, but a modification of the real.

> 'I don't think we should kid ourselves. We haven't *re-created* the past here. The past is gone. It can never be re-created. What we've done is *reconstruct* the past – or at least a version of the past. And I'm saying we can make a better version.'
>
> 'Better than real?'

> 'Why not,'? Wu said. 'After all, these animals are already modified. We've inserted genes to make them patentable, and to make them lysine dependent. And we've done everything we can to promote growth, and accelerate development into adulthood.'
>
> Hammond shrugged. 'That was inevitable. We didn't want to wait. We have investors to consider.'
>
> 'Of course. But I'm just saying, why stop there? Why not push ahead to make exactly the kind of dinosaur that we'd like to see? One that is more acceptable to visitors, and one that is easier for us to handle? A slower, more docile version for our park?'
>
> Hammond frowned. 'But then the dinosaurs wouldn't be real.'
>
> 'But they're not real now,' Wu said. 'That's what I'm trying to tell you. There isn't any reality here.' (Crichton, 1991: 122)

Wu is right. There is no reality in Jurassic Park, but it *seems* like there is, and to a man like Hammond – obsessed with the surface – that is all that matters. The dinosaurs look and feel real; thus, Hammond perceives them as such. It does not matter that, on a cellular (and maybe even philosophical) level, they are not real: Hammond cannot see that and nor can anyone who visits the park. Altering them on that level is acceptable: out of sight, out of mind. Changing them on a visual level, however, is not. When the dinosaurs do not look, sound or feel real, in the way he expects them to, they are not real.

Questions about how we view reality have been an ever-present in science fiction since its conception. A number of authors have created written fiction that asks questions about the limits of perception and how the way we see reality impacts upon reality itself. Cinema has done the same, with the stories growing more complex and expansive with improvements in filmic technology. The advanced special effects used on *The Matrix* trilogy (1999-2003), for example, helped the Wachowskis create a compelling world that genuinely felt different to the world we know. The advancements in immersive technologies such as 3D, IMAX and D-BOX have only added to this sense that a visit the cinema means leaving the real world behind.

Towards the end of the 1980s, Steven Spielberg was starting to express a certain discomfort with that idea. *Empire of the Sun* is not a science fiction film (though its source was written by J.G. Ballard, who made notable contributions to the genre), but it shows its hero having to choose between a difficult reality and a more palatable fantasy when he is put in an internment camp during the Second World War. *Always* is another example, as Spielberg shows the consequences of living a life without responsibility. The film's lead character – irresponsible aerial firefighter Pete – returns as a spirit after death and ends the film shrouded in celestial light: a literal fantasy from which he will never escape. Meanwhile, *Hook* presents us with elaborate, intentionally artificial-looking sets that remind us of the distance between reality and the dream world of Neverland. The man who was hailed as the Peter Pan of Hollywood was starting to question the cost of all that fairy dust.

In *Jurassic Park*, Spielberg took these ideas and combined them with those expressed by Crichton in his novel to ask another, more specific and potentially more controversial, question: how much is cinema warping our perception of reality, and what happens when it alters our perception so fundamentally that we cannot tell fact from fiction? With reference to four core moments in the film and a close reading of Spielberg's style throughout his career, this chapter looks at how he answers that question.

## SPIELBERGIAN REALITY

What is cinematic realism for Steven Spielberg? To answer this question, it is necessary to look back to his first encounter with cinema, which came when he was taken to see *The Greatest Show on Earth* by his father Arnold in 1952. Young Steven was excited by the outing, but had misunderstood what was on offer. When the idea of seeing Cecil B. DeMille's famous circus movie was first proposed, he did not realise he was being taken to the cinema. He thought he was being taken to a real-life circus, with real-life lions, elephants and clowns. When none appeared, he was crushed, and spent the film nursing a feeling of disappointment and betrayal.

# CONSTELLATIONS

> So the curtain is open and I expect to see the elephants and there's nothing but a flat piece of white cardboard, a canvas. And I look at the canvas and suddenly a movie comes on and it's *The Greatest Show On Earth*. At first, I was so disappointed, I was angry at my father, he told me he was taking me to a circus and it's just this flat piece of colour... For a while I kept thinking, Gee, that's not fair. I wanted to see three dimensional characters and all this was was flat shadows, flat surfaces... I was *disappointed* by everything after that. I didn't trust anybody... I never felt life was good enough, so I had to embellish it. (in McBride, 2010: 50-51)

Spielberg would eventually come to enjoy the experience, but the initial disappointment seemed to light a fire under the young filmmaker. As he started on his early experiments with cinema, Spielberg wanted to ensure that he never created a film that disappointed his audience like *The Greatest Show on Earth* did him. He wanted to make cinema more immersive, more real – enhancing that 'flat piece of colour' and giving it three-dimensional life. His 1964 film *Firelight* (a prototype for *Close Encounters of the Third Kind* that finds extraterrestrial lights hovering in the skies above Arizona) was the first full-length feature he ever made. Knowing the story needed convincing special effects in order to work, he found ingenious ways to make his vision a reality. Writing for Empire magazine, Ian Freer explains:

> In a sequence where a child (played by Spielberg's sister Nancy) is abducted by a UFO, Spielberg rewound the film in camera, then double exposed it adding a spacecraft created by a lamp with a red gel and glass dishes filled with red 'jello'. The film also featured elaborate stop-motion effects as the army fight aliens in front of a papier-mâché mountain and the scene of disintegration of the body with actor Clark Lohr, photographed in various states of vaporisation, eight frames at a time, the final shot being a plastic skull (Freer, 2015).

The instinct to draw audiences into his movies with worlds that seem tangibly real has played a key role in all his films since, even those that play within the more fantastical realms of genre cinema. On *Duel* and *Jaws*, for example, he fought hard to shoot on location rather than a soundstage in order to build realism. 'I could have shot the movie in the tank, or even in a protected lake somewhere, but it would not have looked the same,' he told Time magazine about *Jaws* (1975).

# Jurassic Park

Similar thinking informed *E.T.*, which makes striking use of Allen Daviau's cinematography to ground its more magical elements and paint a convincing suburban location. 'I wanted the movie to look very realistic,' Spielberg told American Cinematographer in 1982, 'meaning that if it's 10 o'clock in the morning the sun's going to come directly through both windows and blinds of Elliott's bedroom and they're going to be very hot in contrast to the rest of the room, which would be dark to the taste of the kids' (Turner, 1983). Hungry sharks, malevolent trucks and friendly aliens may be the subjects of these films, but the contexts in which they exist are very much grounded in verisimilitude. They have to be to make them come alive like Spielberg wants.

His cinema is not simply about injecting reality into fantasy though; it is also about incorporating creative licence in historical fact. *Schindler's List* and *Saving Private Ryan* stand out as Spielberg's most obviously 'realistic efforts', but both are heavily influenced by representations of reality rather than objective reality itself. The D-Day sequence in *Saving Private Ryan* was informed by Robert Capa's famous sequence of photographs 'The Magnificent Eleven', which are blurred and out of focus, and so have an air of cinematic editorialising to them: they feel real because their lack of polish tell us they are real. Meanwhile, on *Schindler's List*, Spielberg used black-and-white film stock instead colour in an effort to replicate our remembrance of the Holocaust rather than the actual reality of it. 'I think black and white stands for reality. I don't think colour is real. I think certainly colour is real to the people who survived the Holocaust, but to people who are going to watch the story for the first time, I think black-and-white is going to be the real experience for them,' he said. 'My only experience with the Holocaust has been through black-and-white documentaries' (Schleier, 1994).

In both cases, Spielberg subtly alters the reality of the event through his mise-en-scène in order to shift it more in line with the audience's perception of the event. It is no different than Hammond and his dinosaurs. The dinosaurs are real because they line up with our perception of the reality of a dinosaur, regardless of whether that perception is correct or of what is happening beneath the surface. *Schindler's List* feels real because it lines up with our perception of the reality of the Holocaust, regardless of whether that perception reflects true reality or of what cinematic

49

tricks Spielberg is utilising. By taking this approach, Spielberg successfully turns *The Greatest Show on Earth* into a real circus, and cinema into real life. Whether historical fact or fantastical fiction, the 'flat piece of colour' has disappeared and been replaced by a vibrant, living, three-dimensional world.

In this sense, Spielberg's vision of cinematic reality is defined by a total symbiosis between the audience and the events on screen. It is a topic he has spoken about in a number of interviews. Describing the audience as 'my bosses' (in Taylor, 1992: 12), Spielberg has always worked to 'involve [them in the film] as much as I can so they no longer think they're sitting in an audience' (in Baxter, 1997: 23). In a separate interview, he went further, adding that 'making movies is an illusion, a technical illusion that people fall for. My job is to take that technique and hide it so well that never once are you taken out of your chair and reminded of where you are' (in Taylor, 1992: 40). The camera is his magic wand in this cinematic magic trick, and he has used it in a number of ways to generate the visceral bond he seeks. Critic Frederick Wasser outlines a few of these methods, noting the most prominent as:

> 1) subjective point of view shots extended in time (*Duel*); 2) shocking change of image scale (the shark emerges in *Jaws*); 3) overwhelming action left, right and centre (crowd scenes in *Jaws*); 4) dimensional sound effects (*Raiders of the Lost Ark*); 5) bathing the audience in light (God's light in *Close Encounters of the Third Kind*); 6) and much later he used a chaotic hand-held camera (*Schindler's List*); 7) computer enhancement (*Jurassic Park*); and 8) desaturated colour (*Saving Private Ryan*) to overwhelm the spectators. (Wasser, 63)

Other critics have produced their own insights. In separate video essays, Phillip Brubaker ('Spielberg/Suspense', 2017) and Adam Tinius ('Spielberg: How to Introduce Characters', 2017) investigate Spielberg's technique of foregrounding objects in order to build tension and his method of introducing characters respectively: 'This style of filmmaking takes a passive audience member, and makes them an active participant,' Tinius explains. 'It makes them sit up in their chair and pay attention.' Going deeper, Tony Zhou in 'The Spielberg Oner' (2014) puts the focus on Spielberg's long takes, which Zhou argues aim to 'remain invisible' so the audience does not have their immersion in the film broken. Meanwhile Ken Provencher ('The Spielberg

Touchscreen', 2016) explores how Spielberg emphasises physical touch and 'objects like remote controls, other hands, faces, books, photographs, maps, buried objects, windows and the display screens on electronic devices like televisions and computer monitors. When we see characters demonstrate a tangible connection to objects that also advance a film's narrative, we become, like the characters, active reactors.' All these techniques help draw the audience in to characters, themes and narrative, making them feel a part of the film and not just viewers of it.

Most importantly of all is the so-called Spielberg Face. Suggested by Matt Patches and explored further in a 2011 video essay by Kevin B. Lee, the Spielberg Face is a shot, or series of shots, Spielberg has used in a number of his films. The technique captures the face of a character (or characters) in close-up as they gaze at an off-screen space with a look of awestruck delight. Lee explains:

> If there is one recurring image that defines the cinema of Steven Spielberg, it is the Spielberg Face. Eyes open, staring in wordless wonder in a moment where time stands still, but above all, a childlike surrender in the act of watching: both theirs and ours. It's as if their total submission to what they're seeing mirrors our own. The face tells us that a monumental event is happening. In doing so, it also tells us how we should feel. If Spielberg deserves to be called the master of audience manipulation then this is his signature stroke (Lee, 2011).

Lee argues that *Close Encounters* represents the moment 'Spielberg [discovers] the full power of The Face' (Lee, 2011), and he has used it in significant moments throughout his career, most notably in *E.T.*, *Empire of the Sun* and the Indiana Jones films. The aim, as Lee notes, is to draw the audience in by mirroring their response to the film within the film itself. But, as Nigel Morris notes, the end of *Close Encounters* also resembles a studio set (2007: 14). This is another key Spielbergian technique, in which he replicates the act of creating or watching a film by laying out scenes as if they are sets or cinemas. The technique could be termed the Spielberg View. *Close Encounters*, *Raiders of the Lost Ark* and *E.T.* feature conclusions in which characters gather around a point of wonder and either watch (as in *Close Encounters* and *E.T.*) or refuse to watch (as in *Raiders*). The Mothership, E.T.'s ship and the Ark of the Covenant are the points of wonder, here representing a film; Neary and the scientists,

Elliott and friends, and Indy and Marion are the audience, and they, of course, represent us. As we watch characters watch an event or object, they become our proxy in the fictional space of the film and so our perception mirrors their perception. We are entirely aligned with them, not just passive audience members viewing the action, but active human beings who are as much a part of the film as the characters are.

Lee and Morris are significant influences upon this chapter and the aforementioned techniques underline the effectiveness and totality with which Spielberg goes about creating his immersive realities. We do not just accept his worlds as real because of what is up on screen (the lighting, cinematography, location, and filmstock Spielberg used so persuasively on *Jaws*, *E.T.*, *Schindler's List*, etc.), but *how* we are seeing what is up on screen (composition, camera angle, camera movement). Again, we are chained to our perception and the end result is the eradication of the 'flat piece of colour' separating us from the film. Audience and characters exist in one world, a world that may not necessarily be real by an objective measure of the word, but which nonetheless *feels* real to the audience because the symbiosis between us and the characters is so strong. 'I'm probably socially irresponsible and way down deep I don't want to look the world in the eye,' Spielberg told the New York Times in 1982. 'Actually, I don't mind looking the world in the eye, as long as there's a movie camera between us' (Kakutani, 1982). In *Jurassic Park*, however, the movie camera malfunctions.

## SILVER SCREENS AND SPIELBERG FACES

*Jurassic Park* finds Spielberg critiquing his relationship with cinematic reality and audience perception in order to build something new: a vision of reality where the lens is cracked. To achieve this, he makes use of both the Spielberg Face and the Spielberg View, as well as nods to the entertainment industry through the dialogue and narrative, in order to draw attention to them. By doing this, he achieves the exact opposite of what he had previously been seeking. Instead of removing the 'flat piece of colour', he puts it back in, reminding us that we are watching a film and ultimately telling us that film, and the warping of reality that goes with it, comes with consequences that must be understood and adhered to.

He wastes no time in reaching for this goal as he opens with the scene depicting Muldoon and his team of Park workers ushering a raptor into its pen. As well as representing humanity's desire to control nature, the moment is another example of the Spielberg View. The key elements present in the conclusions of *Close Encounters*, *Raiders* and *E.T.* are at play here as well – the source of spectacle is the raptor and the audience is the Park workers – but the effect is very different. There is no sense of wonder like there was in *Close Encounters* and *E.T.*, and even though Spielberg emphasises the horror as he did in *Raiders*, that film plays out very differently. Indy and Marion could close their eyes to the power of the Ark and, by showing such respect, be saved from its wrath. Muldoon and his company cannot; in fact, closing their eyes will only blind them to the dangerous animal they are trying to control and therefore put them in more danger. If those previous scenes positioned the source of wonder, and therefore cinema itself, as an incredible and powerful thing that binds characters and audience together in a joyous community, this one positions it as a source of terror that drives people apart in an atmosphere of mounting anxiety.

Matching this sense of fear is the disconnect that Spielberg builds. The other sequences came at the end of their respective films and they all featured main characters who we had come to know and relate to during the course of the story. We understand their hopes, dreams and desires and so lining up our perception with theirs is quite simple. By positioning this scene at the very start of *Jurassic Park*, Spielberg changes the audience's relationship with it and the people who populate it. We do not know these characters and so cannot relate to them, either right here or during the rest of the film. Indeed, the only one who appears later is Muldoon, and he is a secondary character who is killed off. Unable to connect to the characters, we have no way of connecting to the scene as a whole, and so the Spielberg View fails to achieve what was previously its core task. Our line of perception – our appreciation of the film's reality and therefore our whole relationship with the film – is under threat.

# CONSTELLATIONS

*Figure 7: Spielberg aims to distance the audience in the opening scenes of* Jurassic Park.
*(© Universal Pictures / Amblin Entertainment)*

As the scene develops, Spielberg turns his attentions towards subverting the Spielberg Face. When the raptor crate is craned into place, he shows a handful of Park workers looking up towards it. Again, we see ourselves in their spectatorship, and Spielberg goes further by hinting at cinematic symbolism in the fine details. As Nigel Morris (2007) notes, the workers wear Jurassic Park-branded hard hats and so are designed to reflect the merchandise-hungry audiences that summer blockbusters attract. They are an 'inscribed audience, all in hats with logos, backlit, [who] look intently upwards, the central figure chewing as if devouring popcorn' (Morris, 2007: 194).

Here, though, there is no sense of wonder or delight. In fact, these men seem rather bored: this is just a part of their day job after all. They have done it many times before and they will no doubt do it many times again. If they are an 'inscribed audience' their attitude stands in stark contrast to that of the *actual* audience, who would have filed into the theatre moments before with popcorn buckets full and excitement at fever pitch. So disconnected are we from the events on screen that we cannot even project our own image into these blank shell characters.

Spielberg continues to distance us from the film when we get our first glimpse of a dinosaur. Grant, Sattler, Malcolm and Gennaro arrive on the island and are taken by Hammond to a plain of land where they see a brachiosaur grazing. Amazement dominates and, of course, the Spielberg Face is used to highlight this sense of wonder and inspire it within the audience. But there is more than simple amazement happening here; there is satire too. Lee (2011) notes this moment when commenting on how the manipulation of The Spielberg Face was becoming more apparent by 1993, and indeed the director seems here to be parodying the perfect Spielbergian set-piece by producing a scene so filled with awe, wonder and characters' reactions to those things that it feels borderline ridiculous and over-the-top. It is a self-aware Spielberg Face that adds further layers to a film that repeatedly comments on cinema's commodification of spectacle.

The sequence begins with a moment reminiscent of countless Spielberg Faces before it: Grant notices a point of wonder and Spielberg conceals it from us by slowly pushing in on Grant. Shocked, he quickly removes his hat, stands up and then takes off his sunglasses. This is Spielberg Face #1. He reaches down to Sattler, who is studying a plant and remains oblivious to the events going on around her. Once she sees what Grant sees, we get a second Spielberg Face and she does the same as Grant did: takes off her sunglasses and stands up. Spielberg's camera follows her up and she joins Grant in a Spielberg Face two-shot (the third Spielberg Face) as the pair of them stand slack-jawed in amazement. Finally, we see what they are seeing as Spielberg cuts to a wide shot which features the jeep Grant, Sattler and Hammond arrived in dwarfed against the enormity of a brachiosaur. It is a typical Spielberg Face reveal, but one Spielberg never releases us from.

As Grant and Sattler study the animal, we are at a low angle, looking up towards it so we are still struck with amazement. We then get another Spielberg Face (the fourth) as Malcolm reacts, sitting in the jeep. We then return to Grant and Sattler. They are *still* looking up at the brachiosaur and Spielberg's camera follows their eyeline. Another cut and we are now looking down towards Grant and Sattler, who remain awestruck. The Spielberg Face is still in place and gets a fifth airing when Spielberg cuts to Gennaro, who has been watching on with amazement. 'We're gonna make a fortune with this place,' he says as Williams' music reaches a triumphant peak.

55

# CONSTELLATIONS

*Figure 8: One of the many Spielberg Faces used during the brachiosaur scene. (© Universal Pictures / Amblin Entertainment)*

It is a line that explicitly touches on the commodification of wonder that this scene explores.

Another cut and another Spielberg Face (number six) as Malcolm laughs to himself, struggling to process what he is seeing, before we go back to Grant and Sattler who are told by Hammond that the Park has a T- Rex. More slack jaws, more amazement, more Spielberg Faces. 'Welcome to Jurassic Park,' says Hammond as Spielberg returns to Grant, who gazes across the plain with yet another look of amazement (that Spielberg returns to twice more before the scene's end) to more dinosaurs. 'How'd you do this?' he asks. 'I'll show you,' comes Hammond's response. Like a director filming a scene, he seems to have orchestrated the whole event, ensuring that every moment is carefully planned for maximum impact, just as every moment (and every Spielberg Face) is carefully planned by Spielberg. If the opening sequence was about exposing cinematic illusion through disconnection, this one does the same through over-familiarity. The Spielberg Face has been used so much that we cannot avoid seeing it for what it is: a cinematic stunt.

## I'LL SHOW YOU

Having established the manipulation, Spielberg then outlines the process for creating it with a run of four sequences that explain how Hammond made the dinosaurs, beginning in the Park's Visitors' Centre, which is still a work-in-progress and is teeming with construction workers: an allusion to the pre-production work that goes into the making of a film. Next, Grant, Sattler, Malcolm, Hammond and Gennaro enter a small screening room, which again reminds the audience of filmmaking: the room resembles the kind of theatre in which filmmakers view rough cuts of their movies (or a "part theme park simulator, part movie theatre," as Morris (2007: 196) notes). Hammond introduces a short film that explains the bio-engineering process and which includes a preamble between the flesh-and-blood Hammond and a virtual Hammond, who is on screen in a pre-recorded sequence. The two Hammonds interact, but the real Hammond forgets his lines, again exposing the artifice of the scene.

The short continues, and another layer of non-reality is added: a cartoon character called Mr. DNA (voiced by Greg Burson), who interacts with the short's live action elements. As the character details the cloning process, Spielberg cuts to Malcolm and Sattler, who look on with amusement, and then we push in on Grant, the camera sitting below his eyeline, a light shimmering just above his head. The Spielberg Face is in full effect, but it is again a Spielberg Face designed to remind us of what we are doing: watching a movie of someone watching a movie. If cinema is indeed 'an illusion' that he has hitherto worked to conceal, Spielberg here fans away the smoke, smashes the mirror and tells the audience exactly how the magic trick is performed during this run of scenes. Everything is an act, everything is a fake.

The tour continues and the group moves on to the second scene, which is set in a laboratory. Having told us how the dinosaurs are created, Spielberg now shows us that process in action, like a behind-the-scenes featurette released before the film's premiere and designed to whet our appetite for the spectacular special effects that lie ahead. The scientists here represent the special effects artists used on major blockbusters such as *Jurassic Park*, and Hammond – as he does throughout – represents the eager director, delighted to be seeing his vision coming into reality.

His determination to be 'at the birth of every creature on this island' and his coddling of the new-born raptor as if it were a baby not only shows his desire to control the nature he has created, but also his intention to impose his vision of reality on the world. Just as the Hammond of the book believed the dinosaurs are real because they look real, the Hammond of the film believes the baby raptor is harmless because it looks harmless. How could such a small creature possibly cause any trouble?

We are again being reminded that everything we are seeing is just a film, and that the control films exert over our perception of reality can backfire in dangerous ways. When the topic of conversation switches to population control, Malcolm questions Hammond's ability to maintain his iron grip over Isla Nublar, and insists that reality will eventually puncture the fantasy he has created: 'Life,' he insists, 'finds a way.' He is eventually proven right and a note of pre-emptive caution is sounded at the end of the scene, when Spielberg employs what could be described as an early example of an 'Anti-Spielberg Face', a style Lee describes in his essay as a face of 'innocence lost, witnessing unspeakable horrors' (Lee, 2011). Beginning on a point of wonder (the new-born raptor that Grant is holding), rather than ending on it, Spielberg cuts to Grant's face as he confirms the animal's species and regards it with dread. The reality and danger of the situation are slowly starting to dawn on him – and us.

A piercing screech (again designed to disorientate and disconnect the audience) introduces us to the third scene in this sequence, which takes place at the raptor pen we saw in the film's opening. The scene shows the raptors being fed, as a cow is lowered into the pen and seized upon by the creatures. Just as he did in the opening sequence, Spielberg keeps the raptors out of view, instead focusing on the human characters, who look on disgusted in a series of low-angle shots. Now the characters have seen how the dinosaurs are made, Hammond's control over their perception is shattered and reality has dawned, causing the old man to look towards his guests with concern. The feeling of disgust is extended to the audience, whose disconnect through Spielberg's approach is complete. The dinosaurs are fake, we now know, as is the sense of wonder they generate in us. But the terror they can inflict is very real indeed.

## SOMETHING REAL

With the Park's power out and the dinosaurs free to leave their pens, control is lost, chaos reigns and Isla Nublar finally becomes a real Jurassic landscape, not just a fabrication of one. Just as he framed control of perception through a cinematic lens, Spielberg frames the chaos that emerges when control fails cinematically as well, with many of the remaining sequences alluding to cinema specifically and entertainment in general. Look, for example, at the descent of the ruined car down the tree, which plays like a theme park ride that has gone horribly wrong; Tim and Grant have to scramble to the floor before the car crushes them. When chaos rules in Jurassic Park, reality itself, as well as nature, strikes back, using the tools of our own warped perception against us.

This motif is strongest in the film's most famous scene: the T-Rex's attack on Tim and Lex. It is *Jurassic Park*'s standout sequence. Arriving around half-way through the film, it marks the moment Spielberg has been building to and represents the story's turning point. From here, the fate of the Park is sealed and characters start developing towards their end point, with Grant experiencing the most dramatic change. The scene mostly takes place in the dark, but despite this it represents the most impactful view of one of the dinosaurs that the film offers – and that is down to how Spielberg uses it to speak to the audience.

If the first half of the film unpicks Spielberg's immersive style, the T-Rex attack actively condemns the audience for falling for it. The scene is simple in its set up. The tour cars stop on a stretch of road outside the T-Rex paddock. One car is occupied by Tim, Lex and Gennaro, while Grant and Malcolm are in the car behind. The two cars are in plain view of each other, with the occupants able to clearly see the other car. It is a classic Spielberg View set up, with viewers (the occupants of the two cars) and a point of wonder (the Rex).

We alternate between these two cars during the course of the scene. In its first half, we are primarily with Tim, Lex and Gennaro. Gennaro is nodding off to sleep, Lex is fanning herself to cool down and Tim is playing with night-vision goggles. Slowly it becomes evident that the T-Rex is in the vicinity as the ground starts to shake and ripples appear in a glass of water. It is a typical slow Spielbergian build-up, but The

## CONSTELLATIONS

Spielberg Faces we see are not ones of anticipation and wonder, as we might expect, but of fear and dread: Gennaro glances in a rear-view mirror trying to convince himself that the shaking is the power coming back on, while Tim looks at the water and nervously draws his sister's attention to it. Moments such as these work to draw us in to Tim and Lex's predicament, giving us an understanding of how vulnerable they are.

*Figure 9: Spielberg uses Tim and Lex's vulnerability to condemn Grant for his passivity. (© Universal Pictures / Amblin Entertainment)*

Throughout this slow build-up, Spielberg cuts back to Grant and Malcolm, who are largely oblivious in the other car. In-keeping with his dislike of children, Grant shows the least concern; he opens the scene by checking in with Gennaro, but not Tim and Lex. 'I didn't ask,' he says when Malcolm wonders if they are okay. 'Why wouldn't they be?' He later nonchalantly gathers rain water in a canister to drink and when the pressure gets too much for Gennaro, he simply watches impassively. 'Now where does he think he's going,' he asks as the lawyer flees to a nearby toilet. Shortly after, the T-Rex rips the fences around its paddock down and stomps out onto the road.

By cutting between the events in the two cars, Spielberg juxtaposes the sense of dread the children feel with the lack of concern shown by Grant and Malcolm. Grant has become so seduced by the Park's wonder that he cannot see the looming danger right in front of him – and we are the same. He, like us, is sitting and watching, almost waiting for something incredible to happen, just as we are. And as the Rex moves out of its paddock, Spielberg makes the connection more explicit with a shot that is positioned behind and between the two men, who sit silhouetted and enraptured by the sight in front of them. With the headlights of the car illuminating the Rex like a projector and the windscreen resembling a screen, the shot looks like the inside of a cinema, with Grant and Malcolm firmly installed as the audience. It is a true Spielberg View moment.

*Figure 10: The T-Rex is shot within a symbolic cinema screen during its escape. (© Universal Pictures / Amblin Entertainment)*

We are now firmly aligned with Grant and Malcolm, and Spielberg continues to condemn Grant for his apathy. With his superior knowledge of the T-Rex, Grant whispers to Malcolm that neither of them should move; the beast's vision being based on movement. However, Lex and Tim are unaware of this, and in her desperation Lex turns a flashlight on to see better, thereby drawing the Rex's attention. Had Grant shown more interest in the children's welfare earlier in the scene, had he been less awestruck by the dinosaurs during the rest of the film, perhaps the terror that will now be inflicted on the kids could have been avoided. The fantasy that the Park represents has blinded him.

As the scene continues, the Rex is relentless in its attacks, and the children scream for their lives. If the Rex was the point of wonder earlier in the scene, now it has become a point of horror. In the other car, Grant and Malcolm continue to watch, Spielberg even working in a joke as Malcolm wipes away condensation from the windscreen to see the attack more clearly. These are Spielberg Faces and this is a Spielberg View, and while we feel drawn in the result is repulsion as much as excitement. Having experienced the children's terror by being in the car with them at the start of the scene, we do not want to sit in awe any more. We want action to be taken – we want Grant to save Tim and Lex.

Eventually he does, but Spielberg's point is already made. Both character and audience are conjoined, as they often are in Spielberg's cinema, but here it is by something negative and critical. The cinematic fantasies Spielberg had engaged with in previous films and the techniques he had used to draw people in to them, to make them see the unreal as real, are inherently dangerous, blinding the characters in his films and the audiences watching them. The only solution is to break free and take action, as Grant does by distracting the Rex.

Here, and in all the other scenes referenced in this chapter, Spielberg poses the same question to us. Can we, as audience members, question the role of filmic fantasies (and Spielberg's fantasies specifically) in our lives and make the same kind of difference?

# CHAPTER 3: DINOSAURS EAT MAN

Dinosaurs may rule the Earth, but *Jurassic Park* is very much the domain of men. Of the film's ten major characters, only two are women (Ellie Sattler and Lex), and when the story begins, they have relatively little power. Sattler plays a secondary role to Grant, and Lex is a screaming damsel in distress whose naivety in switching on a flashlight attracts the near-fatal attentions of the T-Rex. While it is true that all the dinosaurs within the Park are female, this is actually the result of patriarchal dominance rather than a display of feminine superiority. There are no male dinosaurs because Hammond and his team want to remove any possibility of the animals breeding in the wild. Isla Nublar is a man's world, where masculinity controls femininity.

As the film progresses, of course, this changes. The Park's technology malfunctions, the dinosaurs defy their design, evolve and breed, and Sattler and Lex save the day, returning power to the Park and restoring its security systems. The men, on the other hand, suffer. Four are killed (Nedry, Gennaro, Muldoon and Arnold), Malcolm is badly wounded, Hammond sees his dream destroyed, and Grant is forced to re-evaluate his approach to life. 'Dinosaurs eat man, woman inherits the Earth,' says Sattler in a statement she intends as light humour, but which turns out to be prophetic.

Even beyond its numerous gruesome deaths, *Jurassic Park*'s treatment of masculinity revolves specifically around violence. Building portraits of men who seize control through violent means and are punished for their efforts through even more violent ends, Spielberg explores how patriarchal dominance and masculine power are synonymous with such brutality and what men can do to break free of it – if indeed they can do anything at all. This chapter will explore how he does this by looking at his previous films, the bullying he experienced while growing up and the masculine binaries he has created to explore that bullying.

## THE SPIELBERG MAN

Only four of Spielberg's films to date have foregrounded women in lead roles – *The Sugarland Express* (1974), *The Color Purple*, *The BFG* and *The Post* (2017). The focus has instead fallen on the dynamics between men and, in particular, fathers and sons. This has given rise to suggestions that his films espouse patriarchal values, but when explored in the greater context of Spielberg's life and career, such readings are rendered problematic, if not entirely inaccurate. As explored in this book's introduction, Spielberg used his creativity to work through his childhood fears, and he did the same with his sense of masculinity. Dubbed 'Spielbug' because of his sticky-out ears, protruding nose and bulging Adam's Apple, Spielberg was, in his own words, 'a wimp in a world of jocks' as a child (Sragow in Friedman and Notbohm, 2000: 109). He had friends, but they 'were all like me. Skinny wrists and glasses. We were all just trying to make it through the year without getting our faces pushed into the drinking fountain' (in McBride, 2010: 68-69).

These attempts would not always succeed, and as he grew desperate, Spielberg turned to more unusual techniques to change his physical appearance and gain the respect he sought. 'I used to take a big piece of duct tape and put one end on the top of my nose and the other end as high up on my forehead line as I could,' he has explained. 'I had this big nose. My face grew into it, but when I was a child, I was very self-conscious about my schnozz. I thought if you kept your nose taped up that way, it would stay... like Silly Putty' (in McBride, 2010: 69). It never did.

The sporting arena, where strength and physicality are so important, made his sense of inadequacy even worse. 'He would participate, but we would kind of tease him about not being able to throw a football or catch very well,' childhood friend Scott MacDonald told Joseph McBride (2010: 61). On one occasion, as remembered by MacDonald's brother Sandy, 'someone got boxing gloves, and we made a ring between our two houses. When it was Stevie's turn, he got hit and ran away. He got a bottle of ketchup from his house and every time he was hit, he'd pour ketchup on himself. He had it all over his clothes and hair' (McBride, 2010: 61). Spielberg was using entertainment to distract from his perceived lack of masculine prowess.

His experiences at school were mirrored at the Eagle Scouts, where he excelled in most areas, except for the physically demanding ones. 'Steve couldn't do the obstacle course,' remembers friend Tim Dietz. 'That was the only thing he couldn't do to get Eagle Scout' (McBride, 2010: 78). Spielberg also sought to protect those who he believed were being singled out. Charles Carter, another fellow Scout, told McBride:

> A guy named Rechwald had his pants down taking a crap. Rechwald was an underling in the pecking order; I think he was a little obese. Spielberg intervened because we were torturing Rechwald with a flashlight – everybody was shining lights on Rechwald, exposing him and chuckling at him. Spielberg got mad because they were embarrassing him. I think we tortured Steve a little bit [for protesting] – not seriously, we were just kids. But they laid off on Rechwald. I didn't think much about it at the time, but looking back, I was impressed. Most kids didn't stand up against peer pressure. He did. He took a stand. (2010: 78)

The image of the young Steven Spielberg that emerges from these stories is one of a boy who felt uncomfortable in his own masculinity and who disliked seeing others bullied for their masculine deficiencies in the way that he himself was. When he got older, the pranks he used to cope with this evolved into filmic storytelling, and it is telling that his early endeavours were in genres traditionally associated with masculinity – science-fiction (*Firelight*), Westerns (*The Last Gunfight*), Action (*The Last Train Wreck*, 1957) and War (*Fighter Squad, Escape to Nowhere*, 1962) – and that he has so often returned to those genres in his professional career. Not content with real world masculinity, Spielberg reconstituted it through fiction.

This continued when he turned professional. Many of Spielberg's early movies play on the dynamics between weak men and their alpha male counterparts. As such, they can be loosely termed 'bully films'. Speaking about *Duel* to Susan Lacy in 2017, Spielberg explained: 'My early themes always had the underdog being pursued by indomitable forces of both nature and natural enemies, and that person has to rise to the occasion to survive. A lot of that comes just from the insecurities I felt as a kid and how that bled over into the work. I was always the kid with the big bully, and *Duel* was my life in the schoolyard. The truck was the bully, and the car was me.' (Lacy, 2017)

Spielberg's 'bully films' foreground everyman characters – 'Mr Everyday Regular Fellas', as he himself has called them (Tuchman in Friedman and Notbohm, 2000: 50). These characters are often positioned as weak and Spielberg seeks to play them off against a stronger counterpart. The weak heroes see an element of themselves reflected in their strong enemies, and must challenge themselves to become strong too, without ever actually becoming the bully they oppose. Look, for example, at the heroes of *Duel* and *Jaws*. David Mann (*Duel*) and Martin Brody (*Jaws*) are adrift in the world they have been thrown into. Mann, a suburban husband who is failing at work and unable to defend his wife from the sexual advances of other men, needs to adapt to the inhospitable landscape of the American desert. Pursued by the malevolent, masculine-coded truck, he has no option but to do so.

The aquaphobic Brody, meanwhile, is intensely uncomfortable around the waters of Amity: a serious deficiency for a man in charge of the police force in this seaside town. Here, the shark, the town's mayor Larry Vaughan (Murray Hamilton) and alpha male veteran fisherman Quint (Robert Shaw) are the bullies posing a threat that our weakling hero must step up to and overcome. When he fails (an early scene has him succumbing to Vaughan's insistence that the beaches are kept open, despite Brody knowing that a shark is in the water) it leads to a boy's death and a humiliating public slap from the child's mother. Brody has failed in a masculine battle of wits and been punished for it.

In both cases, Mann and Brody ultimately succeed in becoming stronger men, but while they save the day, they do not become alpha male bullies like their opponents. Unable to physically outmanoeuvre the truck driver, Mann outsmarts him, plucking up courage enough to enter into a game of chicken before leaping out of his car just as the truck ploughs into it and over the edge of a cliff. Brody, meanwhile, confronts Vaughan after yet another preventable beach attack, outlives Quint, whose hyper-masculine ego-mania leads to his death, and destroys the shark just as the situation seems to be at its most desperate. His ingenuity in spotting a gas canister in the beast's mouth is the turning point, with Spielberg again marking his hero's intelligence and bravery as being more important than physical strength.

Spielberg underlines the dangers of dominant masculinity by making his bully characters seem monstrous through visual distortion and displacement. The truck driver, whose name we never learn, face we never see and motivation we never grasp, is the most obvious example, but it is also seen with Quint, who is introduced through the off-screen sound of fingernails scraping down Amity town hall's blackboard. The uniformly male government agents depicted in *E.T.* are no different. Concealed by shadow, smoke or, during the invasion of Elliott's home, hazmat suits that make them seem more alien than E.T. itself, they are a force to be feared and stand in stark contrast to the innocence of the children and their otherworldly friend. Underlining the link between masculinity and fragmented personalities, the leader of this group (Peter Coyote's Keys) is signified for the majority of the film only by a pair of phallic keys that dangle from his belt towards his groin area. Only once Elliott comes to understand this seeming bully as a force for good who longed for a friend like E.T. when he himself was a child do we see his face and connect with him. For Spielberg, masculinity is a dehumanising disguise, shifting in order to con, coerce and control. Only by shedding it does a man become human.

Even when he does not visually distort his dangerous men, Spielberg seeks to visually call out their brutality and its links to masculinity in other ways. World War II comedy *1941* depicts a number of violent, dominating or deranged men who Spielberg satirises: the insane Wild Bill Kelso (John Belushi), the *Dumbo*-loving General Stillwell (Robert Stack), the sex-crazed Captain Birkhead (Tim Matheson). However, he reserves particular venom for Chuck 'Stretch' Sitarski (Treat Williams), a vicious and controlling soldier who is locked in a love triangle with the pretty Betty (Diane Kay) and nerdy restaurant dishwasher Wally (Bobby Di Cicco).

More than any other character, Stretch is *1941*'s bully. During one of the film's standout sequences, Wally and Betty take part in a dance competition that Wally has been in intense training for. When Stretch appears with sights set on Betty, the dance escalates into a fight, as Stretch relentlessly pursues Wally in an effort to knock him out and claim Betty. The sequence ends with Spielberg pushing in on Stretch in a shot that ends with him in a medium close-up. Fists clenched, the character breaks the fourth wall by looking directly into the camera as a neon American flag is situated behind him. For Spielberg, Stretch's desire to wipe out his competition, undermine a traditionally feminine activity such as dancing, and gain control over Betty is linked to America's military endeavours. Toxic masculinity is as inherently violent as global conflict.

## CONSTELLATIONS

The Indiana Jones films shift the bully binary model slightly. Indy is hardly a weak character, and takes a principled stand against bullies – but Spielberg pushes him to the ends of his morality (and sometimes beyond) in the face of them. In *Raiders of the Lost Ark*, he foreshadows Belloq's suggestion that he and Indy aren't so dissimilar by shrouding the character in darkness during the opening sequence. Later in the same sequence, Spielberg captures him in wide shots to create a sense of distance and close-ups to generate distortion. When we finally see his face, it comes after he has whipped a pistol out of the hands of one of his treacherous guides. He steps out of the shadows and John Williams' music takes a dark turn, underlining the character's ambiguous nature. Later, his fraught relationship with Karen Allen's Marion (who he met when they were young and seemingly took advantage of) is symbolised by his entrance into her Nepalese bar. Spielberg captures Marion in a wide shot slightly to the left of frame. Occupying the centre of the frame is Indy's shadow, which is projected across the majority of the wall and lurks over Marion like Dracula over a victim. The challenge for Indy is to reject his darker instincts, which he does by closing his eyes to the Ark's opening and therefore surviving its wrath.

Spielberg steers the character even closer to the bully image in *Temple of Doom*. A prequel to *Raiders*, *Temple* positions Indy as an arrogant playboy who appears in a James Bond-style tuxedo in the film's opening, pursues 'fortune and glory' at any cost and is seen during the finale with a machete in his hand and muscular body rippling under a torn shirt – a paragon of physical strength. Yet while Indy embodies the bully image visually, Spielberg goes to great lengths to undermine and punish him through the narrative. He is frequently wrong ('So long, Lao Che,' he says triumphantly as he unknowingly boards one of the gangster's planes) and is repeatedly forced to consume dangerous substances that threaten to change him: poison, disgusting food, black liquid that puts him into a trance and alters his personality. The Indiana Jones of *Temple of Doom* actually *does* become a bully, but he is one Spielberg does not approve of, repeatedly mocks and tries his utmost to redeem. By the film's end, the 'fortune and glory' he once sought has been replaced by an understanding that community and togetherness are more valuable than a dominant masculinity that seeks to assert control.

## CHAOS AND CONTROL

If traditional bully films are about strengthening weak characters without making them toxic, and Indiana Jones pushes its hero to the borders of bullying toxicity, *Jurassic Park* evolves the model still further by making seemingly good characters toxic from the outset and trying to redeem them. Traditional and destructive forms of masculinity are not just limited to physically strong men, whose morality is questioned through actions and visual signifiers. The control, violence and domination those characters seek has seeped into every kind of man, whether that's the alpha masculinity of Muldoon, the 'wimps in a world of jocks' that Nedry and Gennaro represent, or Hammond and Grant, the film's ostensible heroes who Spielberg pushes perilously into villain territory. The cure for this is the abandonment of control and the admission of chaos into one's life, which is here represented through Grant's formation of a surrogate family with Tim and Lex. In *Jurassic Park*, those characters who cannot make this kind of transition suffer and die.

The most unpleasant deaths are reserved for two characters who, in previous years, may have even been the heroes of *Jurassic Park*. Gennaro and Nedry are the kind of nerdy, physically inferior men Spielberg made heroes of in *Duel*, *Jaws* and *1941*, but there is no such underdog triumphalism here as he represents their pursuit of power through money. After seeing the park, Gennaro says that he and Hammond could 'charge anything we want – two thousand a day, ten thousand a day – and people will pay it' before patronisingly suggesting that there could be 'a coupon day' to make it accessible to less wealthy families. This ignoble behaviour continues later when he abandons Tim and Lex to the T-Rex. His death is that rare thing in a Spielberg film: a comedic one that the audience is supposed to laugh at and enjoy, not be morally affected or horrified by. It is a far cry from the novel, in which the more likeable Gennaro survives.

Nedry, meanwhile, is similarly obsessed with dominance and wealth: as discussed in the previous chapter, he has seemingly unlimited control of the park and sacrifices everyone's safety for the opportunity to make money. Crichton outlined motives for his betrayal in the book (he was tricked by Hammond and InGen, and plans to steal the embryos as an act of revenge), but Spielberg and Koepp here strip them away, suggesting instead that 'money problems' (never detailed but presumably of his own creation) inspire his actions (such ambiguity contributes to the lack of sympathy afforded to Nedry and the sense of fat-shaming addressed previously). These are nasty, venal men with no redeeming features and by positioning the kind of hero we saw in his 'bully films' as villains, Spielberg underlines just how corrupt masculinity has become. Even traditional good guys are bad.

Further subversion can be seen in Muldoon, the first character of any consequence the film introduces us to. We meet him when he is overseeing the unloading of a velociraptor into its pen and while he may not be built in quite the same way as other action heroes, we are asked to accept him as that kind of controlling presence. Armed and physically strong, he stops the film dead with his mere figure, Spielberg pushing in on him to give him a greater sense of power. As such, we seehim as the kind of character who will secure our safety and prevent any problems; nothing could possibly go wrong around him. Except, of course, it does: the raptor disrupts the loading process and a Park worker is killed. Immediately, Spielberg has defied our expectations of what we should expect from this seeming paragon of male control. We are not secure. He does not have all the answers. Traditional masculinity will not save us.

*Figure 11: Spielberg's composition gives Muldoon a sense of power that he later undermines. (© Universal Pictures / Amblin Entertainment)*

# Jurassic Park

As the film progresses, Spielberg employs a certain cruel irony in his treatment of Muldoon, who we come to see as anything but the typical action hero we took him for in the opening scene. He understands the dangers of the Park, is smart and level-headed, has a clear sense of responsibility and chastises Hammond for some of his glaring safety oversights ('I told you we needed locking mechanisms on the cars!'). Unlike most action heroes of the time, he is happy to work as part of a wider team to get the Park back online and, while Hammond shows his sexist side by suggesting that he and not Sattler should venture into the jungle to restore the power ('I'm a... and you're a...'), Muldoon forms an effective partnership with her.

He looks like a typical action hero, but acts like Brody: a grounded 'Mr Everyday Regular Fella' who we can relate to and support. If *Jurassic Park* were a fair moral universe dictated by right and wrong, good and bad, Muldoon would have survived. But it is not. Chaos is the judge, jury and executioner here and control is the punishable crime. By believing he knows enough about the raptors to outwit them, Muldoon seals his fate. During his attempts to restore the power with Ellie, he thinks he has gained the upper hand, cornering one of the dinosaurs and taking aim. But another surprises him, locking him in a trap and attacking. Arnold – another rational man who the film generates empathy for – suffers a similar fate for a similar reason: he, like Muldoon, tried to restore control over the Park, and whoever you are, wherever you fall on the bully binary scale, that is the crime Jurassic Park punishes.

Occupying a unique and complex place on the film's moral scale is Malcolm. He laughs salaciously, wields his knowledge arrogantly, flirts outrageously and is, by his own admission, a womaniser who is 'always on the lookout for the future ex-Mrs Malcolm.' His arrogance is reminiscent of Mayor Vaughan from *Jaws* and his handsomeness of Stretch from *1941* and to underline his dubious morals, Spielberg shrouds the character's face – just as he did Indiana Jones's at the start of *Raiders* – by keeping his eyes behind black sunglasses that he rarely takes off. But while Malcolm may not be a 'good' character by traditional markers of the word, and indeed Spielberg's previous definitions, the director positions him as a hero because he understands the film's true moral message.

From the moment he arrives at the Park, Malcolm identifies its insurmountable problems, expressing fear and shock when he first sees the brachiosaur rather than Grant and Sattler's wonder and delight: 'You did it, you crazy son of a bitch. You really did it!' As the film moves on and the characters discuss the ethics of the Park across a number of scenes, much of his dialogue revolves around his concern over how Hammond's control will inevitably crumble. He expresses this worry though Chaos Theory – the embodiment of the loss of control all the characters need to strive to accept – and while his comments generally fall on deaf ears, they are proven accurate, much to Malcolm's sardonic regret: 'Boy, do I hate being right all the time,' he says as the Rex breaks free.

A 'rock star' (to quote Hammond) he may be, but he is the only character who understands mankind's inability to control chaos, and therefore acts as the film's Jiminy Cricket – an aptly ambiguous conscience for a film that focuses so much on the unconscionable.

## SHEER WILL

Another indicator of Malcolm's complex position within *Jurassic Park*'s moral ecosystem is his outfit. From the moment we first see him to the film's end, Malcolm is dressed head to toe in black, a colour that is of course frequently used to symbolise evil. Malcolm is *not* evil, but unusually for a character in a Spielberg film, he is a cynic, a realist who sees the world for what it truly is. He is contrasted with Hammond, who is dressed entirely in white to mark him as a dreamer, grasping for an ideal that will never become reality. Again, we have another binary and again Spielberg undermines it. Just as Malcolm is not the villain, Hammond is not the hero. His dress code is, itself, an ideal: a self-made image crafted by a man who wants to see himself as a paragon of virtue, the kind of good character Spielberg once made a hero of. In fact, he is anything but.

In adapting the Hammond character from book to screen, Spielberg attracted some criticism for softening his edges. For Crichton, Hammond is a ruthless businessman who ignores the warnings of the scientists he has hired to advise him and refuses to be diverted from his path. His punishment for his hubris is a particularly painful death: he falls down a hill, breaks his ankle and is killed by a pack of compsognathus. Spielberg cast actor/director Richard Attenborough in the role, and some critics have argued that the personal connection (Spielberg seeing himself reflected in his fellow filmmaker) inspired him to create a character who is misguided, rather than downright bad. 'The crotchety, almost dwarfish curmudgeon of the book... had metamorphosed into a jolly Santa Claus whose toys have got out of hand,' writes John Baxter (1997: 378).

While there is some truth in that reading, it is a somewhat shallow one that does little to explore Hammond's depths. Under Spielberg, the character is just as remorseless and relentless as he is under Crichton. He is unsympathetic toward Nedry's financial problems ('they are your problems'), has no qualms about exposing his young grandchildren to the park's dangerous animals and untested security systems, and when Sattler confronts him on his actions, he tells her with thinly-veiled ferocity that 'creation is an act of sheer will.' Spielberg's Hammond is all surface pleasantries with venom sitting beneath: a nicer Hammond, but a no less dangerous one. As Attenborough himself explained:

> I thought the part was fascinating, and quite different from the Hammond in the book. In the book, Hammond really was a bit of a sod – even villainous to a certain point. The screenplay illustrated a man of some ruthlessness and determination, but also considerable charm, who uses that charm and a kind of impresario flair to persuade people. (Shay and Duncan, 1993: 71)

This charm and flair is utilised by Hammond to gain control, and Spielberg explicitly links him to violence and masculinity during the boardroom sequence in which Hammond, Malcolm, Grant, Sattler and Gennaro discuss the ethics of bioengineering. Hammond and Malcolm exchange heated words as Malcolm compares Hammond to 'a kid that's found his dad's gun' and dubs discovery, and, by extension, Hammond's creation of Jurassic Park, 'a violent and penetrative act... the rape of the natural world'. Hammond brushes his concerns aside, but he finds little more support from Grant and Sattler, who only echo Malcolm's points. Sattler argues that the dinosaurs, confused by the environment they are now in, will defend themselves, 'violently, if necessary'. Hammond is taken aback and tries to make light of the situation. 'I don't believe it. I don't believe it,' he says, defeated. 'You're meant to come down here and defend me against these characters, and the only one I've got on my side is the bloodsucking lawyer.' Even in the mundane setting of a corporate boardroom, *Jurassic Park* is riddled with acts of aggression.

This sequence is echoed later when Hammond and Sattler sit in the Visitor Centre's restaurant. With the Park's systems down and the dinosaurs loose, Hammond is totally powerless and reduced to eating the restaurant's ice cream before it melts: the boy who found his father's gun is now the boy who has fled sulking to his bedroom after being reprimanded. Spielberg visually underlines his diminished status by panning across a shelf of Jurassic Park merchandise in the foreground before landing on Hammond, small and meek, in the background: here is the creator dwarfed by his own creation. Sattler lingers on the sidelines and joins Hammond at the table. Another binary is built, with Hammond sitting at one end of the table and Sattler at the other.

As the scene continues Spielberg suggests that Hammond could be on the verge of an epiphany. He opens up to Sattler about his inspiration for Jurassic Park, which evolved from his desire to turn the flea circuses of his youth into something bigger and more tangible. Capturing the moment in a wide two-shot, Spielberg bonds Hammond and Sattler together, but ensures there is a table standing between them. With Hammond's story continuing in a way that suggests he may not be learning a lesson after all, Spielberg starts isolating the characters, breaking with two-shots and moving into singles, first to Sattler and then to Hammond.

Background details confirm Hammond's lack of growth and continued commitment to his controlling and potentially violent behaviour. Behind Sattler, a mural of a herd of herbivores (parasaurolophus) sits, while behind Hammond, there is an eruptingvolcano and dinosaur mural designed to echo Pablo Picasso's painting 'Guernica' (1937), which famously depicts the violent horror of war. Sattler is visually defined by calm and peace, while Hammond is disruption and violence, and when Spielberg cuts to another shot, he intensifies Hammond by framing him at a low angle between two chairs as he says: 'We're over-dependent on automation, I can

*Figure 12: Spielberg frames Hammond against a violent background during his scene with Sattler. (© Universal Pictures / Amblin Entertainment)*

see that now. Now, the next time, everything's correctable.' During this line, Sattler is shot in a similar way as Spielberg shows how Hammond is trying to exert control over her. 'Creation is an act of sheer will,' he says, Spielberg cutting again, this time to a one-shot of Hammond. 'Next time, it'll be flawless.'

Hammond's refusal to learn his lesson is clear, and Sattler turns on him, with Spielberg alternating between close-ups of Hammond and Sattler as he underlines the disconnect the two characters now share.

Sattler: It's still the flea circus. It's all an illusion...

Hammond: When we have control again...

Sattler: You never had control – that's the illusion! I was overwhelmed by the power of this place, but I made a mistake too: I didn't have enough respect for that power. And it's out now. The only thing that matters now are the people we love: Alan and Lex and Tim. John, they're out there and people are dying.

Hammond reflects and seems to concede the ground, but shadows of the old showman remain: 'Spared no expense,' he says when Sattler tries some of the ice cream. He has not really learned his lesson, and he never truly does. When the helicopter leaves the island to take the survivors back to the mainland at the film's end, Hammond is finally forced to acknowledge the death of his dream. He sits motionless and gazes with empty eyes at the egg of amber at the top of his cane: he is stuck in a fantasy of what might have been.

So, Spielberg ends Hammond's journey not on a binary, but a connection: between Hammond and the mosquito in the amber egg. He, like the mosquito, is trapped, a relic of a bygone era. He, like the mosquito, is a bloodsucker, violently penetrating the surface to leech what it needs off something else. The man who once had control over life is now reduced to the same level as the creature he exploited to gain that control.

## EVOLUTION

When we meet him, Alan Grant seems an essentially good man. He is smart, respectful of nature and during the boardroom scene expresses concern about Hammond's actions. He looks to be the typical everyman and Spielberg made changes to the novel to make him less like an action hero. For Crichton, Grant is 'a barrel-chested, bearded man of forty' (1991, 32) who 'measure(s) time in beer' (1991, 33); a description that does not fit Sam Neill.

Before casting Neill, Spielberg considered a number of actors for the role, including his Indiana Jones star Harrison Ford. Casting Ford would have brought the character more in line with Crichton's strong and earthy type, but it would have also upended the binary-breaking narrative the film engages in. Grant should not seem in control, he should not look like the action hero. Crichton's Grant is a man who seems in control without ever trying, but for Spielberg to deconstruct the binaries he has previously used, his Grant must seem like Mann and Brody (lost, confused and trying to find his bravery) before breaking from that mould through violent bids for control that he must ultimately reject. That Spielberg also considered William Hurt and Richard Dreyfuss seems to underline that he wanted one of his Mr Everyday Regular Fellas to play this character who bucks the trend.

Similar to Hammond, this control manifests itself in moments that are marked by indirect violence, but with Grant, Spielberg trains the focus of that violence exclusively on children. This marks another significant change from Crichton's novel, which notes that Grant 'liked kids – it was impossible not to like any group so openly enthusiastic about dinosaurs' (115). Writing about Grant's attitude to children in Sight and Sound (1993), Henry Sheehan goes so far as to suggest that the character actually wants to kill Tim and Lex:

> The two most terrifying scenes in the film revolve specifically around the children's near death at the hands first of a tyrannosaurus rex and then of the velociraptors. But these events also serve to play out the child-murder fantasies of Dr. Grant. Grant's girlfriend, paleobotanist Dr. Ellie Sattler, claims laughingly that the scientist has a phobia about kids, as if it were a bachelor's tic. But the way Neill plays Grant, dark and morose, there doesn't seem anything lighthearted about his disdain for them. (Sheehan, 1993)

*Figure 13: Spielberg visually represents Grant's latent violence during the Badlands sequence. (© Universal Pictures / Amblin Entertainment)*

The first, and most striking, example of this violent disdain comes when Grant is confronted at his Badlands dig by a young boy who is unafraid of raptors and dismissively compares them to 'six foot turkeys'. Angered by the suggestion, Grant outlines an imaginary scenario that ends with the boy being attacked and eaten alive by one of the dinosaurs.

While doing this, Grant acts his story out by using a fossilised raptor claw to literally slash at the boy's belly. It is a moment of surprising violence from a character who is supposed to be the hero of what has been marketed as a family film. He is not so much arguing against the boy's point as trying to make him deathly afraid – of both dinosaurs and Grant himself. Grant's challenge in the film is to rid himself of this latent violence and control.

It does not prove easy though. Grant's violence is so deeply embedded within him that it has physical manifestations: the raptor claw and a blood red bandana he wears around his neck like an ever-present cut-throat hand gesture. By drawing attention to these items, Spielberg is fragmenting the hero of *Jurassic Park* just as he had the villains and morally ambiguous character of *Duel*, *Jaws*, *E.T.* and, more contemporaneously to this film, *Hook*, in which the eponymous appendage provides a potent representation of its villain's violence and masculinity. Spielberg goes even further here though, not only fragmenting Grant and hinting at how he could slip into becoming a bully as he had done before, but fully associating him with killer creatures: the dinosaur predators.

Though we see his affection for the sick Triceratops ('my favourite when I was a kid'), Grant is utterly astonished by the T-Rex in a way he is not by the Trike, spends time quizzing Muldoon about the raptors after being shown their pen, and cradles the hatchling raptor in the lab. Among the many other things it symbolises, the T-Rex's attack on Tim and Lex is a moment of character development, in which Grant finally realises his underlying violence and reacts against it. He is the T-Rex and if he does not turn his life around, he will be the one attacking the kids.

This moment marks the start of Grant's redemption, as he begins to protect Tim and Lex rather than pushing them away. Eventually, they form a surrogate family, and Spielberg underlines this new bond by positioning them and Sattler together in the same frame when the raptors are ready to pounce on them during the finale. It is, of course, a deeply Spielbergian moment that highlights the importance of the family unit, but it also symbolises Grant's abandonment of control, the violence needed to seize it, and the acceptance of chaos into his life.

The link between children and chaos is made explicit during the Badlands sequence. After threatening the boy, Grant discusses plans for the future with Sattler, Grant asking her if she plans on having children.

Sattler: I don't want *that* kid, but a breed of child, Dr. Grant, could be intriguing. I mean, what's so wrong with kids?

Grant: Oh, Ellie, look, they're noisy, they're messy, they're expensive.

Sattler: Cheap... cheap...

Grant: They smell.

Sattler: They do not smell.

Grant: Some of them smell.

Sattler: Oh, give me a break!

Grant: Babies smell!

This dialogue suggests that Grant's attitude towards children does not only come from a place of hatred (though hatred is how it manifests itself), but fear: a fear of their smell, their noise, their cost and their mess. In other words, a fear of the chaos that children bring, and the lack of control Grant can exert over that chaos. The chaos is made real when Tim and Lex arrive and Spielberg has them run into Hammond's arms with such force that the old man falls to the floor. Standing nearby, Sattler smiles and turns to a scowling Grant, who Spielberg positions so far to the right of the frame that he is almost out of it entirely, so desperate is he to avoid the youngsters. Sattler turns back, the smile removed from her face.

Later, when the tour is about to get underway, Grant attempts to avoid the dinosaur enthusiast Tim, but the boy pursues him from car to car, asking questions about his work. Spielberg captures the moment in a long take that emphasises Grant's inability to avoid the boy's relentlessness. Lex is just as persistent. When the group break from the tour to visit the sick Triceratops, Lex grabs Grant's hand and does not let go. Clearly uncomfortable, he tries to wrestle his hand free, but there is no escaping these children.

Adding extra urgency to the need to unburden Grant of his violence, Spielberg dresses Tim in clothes that mirror Grant's: bandana around the neck, blue shirt, khaki shorts. The boy wants to be Grant, and that means everything about him: the

## CONSTELLATIONS

good and the bad. Eradicating Grant's violence will not just save him, it will save Tim as well, and so another subversive bully binary is formed. Tim is the classic Spielberg hero, and Grant – the ostensible hero – is the aggressive bully whose toxic masculinity the boy must resist.

Following the T-Rex attack and the realisation of his latent violence, Grant changes his ways and his new outlook on life is highlighted when he, Tim and Lex take shelter in a tree canopy overlooking a herd of brachiosaurs – the focus on predators now replaced by an association with less ferocious beasts. Indeed, so at home in this new outlook is he that he even tries to communicate with the dinosaurs, cupping his hands together and blowing through them to mimic the animals' calls. Scared that they will attack, Lex asks Grant to stop, and he assures her that they are safe in a kind and gentle manner ('They're not monsters Lex, they're just animals. These are herbivores'). Even when Tim goads his sister, Grant shows no sign of the angry frustration he displayed during the Badlands sequence; here, a simple, calm reprimand ('Tim...') suffices. This is a Grant less focused on control and more comfortable with the chaos that children inevitably bring.

As he moves to sit down and is accompanied by Tim and Lex, Grant is given one last echo of his old life; the raptor claw he put in his pocket is now jabbing against his leg. So far has he moved from his former self that he had forgotten that it was there. He takes it out and briefly regards it, before putting his arm around Tim, his hand and the claw now stretched to the far left of the frame. Lex asks him what he and Sattler will do now that Hammond has essentially made paleontology redundant and Grant admits that they will have to evolve. Another look at the raptor claw follows before he finally decides to let go, throwing the claw to the ground. Spielberg cuts to a close-up of the fossil before moving into the next scene: that featuring Hammond and Sattler in the Visitor Centre restaurant. The message is clear: Grant has changed, Hammond has not. And in the film's final moments, Spielberg shows what happens as a result.

While Hammond ends up locked in his amber egg, forever associated with the control and violence that defined his life, Grant is free. Linking back to Grant's theory that dinosaurs evolved into birds, Spielberg associates him with a flock of birds that fly alongside the helicopter as it escapes the island. No longer dealing exclusively with beings that are long dead and doggedly holding onto the control that this affords him, Grant accepts his role in the world and his inability to dictate it. He truly has evolved; not from paleontologist to ex-paleontologist, or from bully to hero, but into a different kind of man, one able to seek acceptance and peace in the world, not control and dominance over it.

# CONCLUSION: RAIN INSTEAD OF SHINE

Just a few months after *Jurassic Park* appeared, Steven Spielberg released another film, one that stands in marked contrast to that which audiences had lapped up in the summer. *Schindler's List* was a considerably darker, more sombre affair that found its director engaging directly with the Holocaust and his Jewish heritage for the first time. Despite its intense subject matter, the film was a critical and commercial success, and in March 1994 it won Spielberg the Best Picture and Best Director Academy Awards he had coveted throughout his career.

The brace was part of a seven-award windfall that also included Best Adapted Screenplay (Steve Zaillian), Best Original Score (John Williams) and Best Cinematography (Janusz Kamiński) amongst others. Spielberg had hit a career peak, not only redefining the blockbuster with *Jurassic Park*, but also forging a new path for himself with *Schindler's List*'s delicate handling of a highly sensitive subject. A new era dawned. What would he do to follow this remarkable year?

As it happened, he did nothing. At least not behind the camera. After the Oscars, Spielberg took a break from directing and instead focused on expanding his horizons by setting up The Shoah Foundation, which records the testimony of Holocaust survivors for future generations, and establishing the studio DreamWorks SKG alongside David Geffen and Jeffrey Katzenberg. The all-conquering director had become a great mogul and philanthropist, and when he returned to movie-making, he did so with a three-pronged attack that reflected his joint interests in education and entertainment: historical duo *Amistad* (1997) and *Saving Private Ryan* (1998), and a *Jurassic Park* sequel.

*The Lost World: Jurassic Park* (1997) arrived atop a wave of hype, but disappointed upon release and remains one of Spielberg's few widely-acknowledged artistic failures. It takes place four years after the events of *Jurassic Park* and is based on Isla Sorna ('Site B'), an abandoned supply factory on which dinosaurs were bred ready to be shipped to Isla Nublar. With John Hammond's health fading and lawsuits undermining his power, he has lost control of InGen to his nephew, Peter Ludlow

# CONSTELLATIONS

*Figure 14: The end of* Jurassic Park *highlights a shift in Spielberg's approach to his filmmaking. (© Universal Pictures / Amblin Entertainment)*

(Arliss Howard), who hopes to hunt the animals and take them to a new Jurassic Park in San Diego. Hammond wants to put a stop to this and protect Sorna's dinosaurs from further interference, so he enlists a team of experts, including photographer Nick Van Owen (Vince Vaughn) and equipment technician Eddie Carr (Richard Schiff), to document the dinosaurs and prove they are worthy of preservation. He asks Ian Malcolm to join the group too, but the hesitant mathematician only accepts when he learns that behavioural paleontologist (and his girlfriend) Sarah Harding (Julianne Moore) is also on the team.

Malcolm's reluctance seems to reflect Spielberg's own. As initial planning of the film started, he was unsure of whether he would have the time to direct and considered handing the reins over to someone else and acting only as producer. His final decision was informed by two factors. Firstly, he was keen to protect the integrity of the first film after witnessing the three poor *Jaws* sequels that were released after the success of the original. 'Many people think he still had something to do with them,' long-time producing partner Kathleen Kennedy told Premiere magazine's Peter Biskind. 'So there's a proprietary creative interest to protect and ensure the quality' (Friedman and Notbohm, 2000: 197). Secondly, he was looking for a straightforward route back to the director's chair. 'Coming back from those three years of not directing, I didn't want to jump into the deep end of the pool,' Spielberg told Biskind, 'I wanted to step into the shallow end and get used to the water. I wanted to do something familiar'

(Friedman and Notbohm, 2000: 198).

Yet, familiarity breeds contempt. *The Lost World* opens on the Sorna coast, where a wealthy family on a private cruise are enjoying time ashore. Their young daughter wanders away and stumbles upon a pack of Compsognathus, who attack her. Upon seeing her injured daughter, the girl's mother screams and Spielberg uses a drily comedic smash cut to take us from this moment to the sight of Malcolm yawning as he waits for a subway train. Later, as his fellow explorers see dinosaurs for the first time and respond with wonder, Malcolm is sarcastic and dismissive: 'Oh yeah. Oooh, aaah, that's how it always starts. Then later there's running and screaming.' Finally, in the film's third act, Spielberg indulges his love for monster movies when a T-Rex is let loose in San Diego. He references *The Lost World* (1925), *King Kong* (1933) and *Godzilla* (1954) in scenes that seem to be commenting on the repetitive nature of sequels and also feature a cameo from the film's writer David Koepp as a man (dubbed 'Unlucky Bastard' in the credits) who is gobbled up by the Rex.

*The Lost World* is a darkly satirical joke in which Spielberg breaks the fourth wall with even more glee than he did in *Jurassic Park*. No longer does he simply point out cinematic artifice and ask us to question it; he mocks us for ever believing in it, and, in the film's standout action sequence, emphasises its absurdity and juxtaposes it with a sense of cruelty. Restaging the Rex attack from the first film, Spielberg ups the ante to a ridiculous degree by having two Rexes (rather than one) attack a large mobile laboratory (rather than a small car) and push it over the edge of a cliff to create a knowingly literal cliffhanger. The victim here is not a cold and calculated lawyer whose death brings laughter and cheers, but a good man – Eddie – whose demise is brutal, tragic and undeserved: he is torn in half by the Rexes as he tries to save his colleagues. Our enjoyment of the action is therefore undercut even more than it was in *Jurassic Park*. This is a hollow and farcical spectacle that offers no heroic redemption.

Spielberg is no less critical in his depiction of masculinity. Like *Jurassic Park*, *The Lost World* is dominated by men, and only one (Eddie) can be described as unambiguously good. Nick is a self-absorbed poseur whose environmentalism is driven as much by a desire to meet women as it is to further a cause. Big-game

# CONSTELLATIONS

hunter Roland Tembo (Pete Postlethwaite) and his partner Ajay (Harvey Jason) are killers who want to claim a male Rex as a trophy. And Tembo's second-in-command Dieter (Peter Stormare) is needlessly cruel, viciously electrocuting some of the Compsognathus simply to prove his power over them. Hammond is somewhat reformed – turning, in Malcolm's words, from 'capitalist to naturalist' – but remains a flawed figure, still hoping he can control the world around him and putting other people in danger while doing so.

The two most prominent men are, of course, Malcolm and Ludlow, and Spielberg uses them to continue his subversion of the bully binary. Ludlow is the kind of character Spielberg would have turned into a hero earlier in his career – a weak, nerdy man – but he is positioned as the primary villain here. In this sense, he is the Dennis Nedry of *The Lost World*, but something of a reversal of the character: where Nedry is obese, Ludlow is thin; where Nedry is crude and messy, Ludlow is refined and tidy; where Nedry is motivated by a desire to become rich, Ludlow is already rich and motivated by a desire to *increase* his wealth. Both are defined by their relationship with power and control, but again, Spielberg builds a key difference. Nedry creates control through his skills, which enable him to automate the Park; Ludlow seems to lack any identifiable skills and simply steals power from his uncle.

In this way, Ludlow is an even more odious presence than Nedry, and Spielberg repeatedly punishes him by denying him the power he seeks in humiliating and public ways. As he and his team journey through the island for the first time, he suggests they set up camp on what, unknown to him, is a feeding site for the dinosaurs. His ignorance earns him a harsh reprimand from Tembo, who angrily dismisses his thoughts and likens him to a rich dentist on safari. Later, when the men's morale is low, he attempts to inspire them to get back on their feet and resume their path. However, they pay him no attention and only move when asked to do so by Nick, for whom they have far more respect. Humbled, Ludlow cuts a forlorn figure, completely adrift in a world he cannot fully lay claim to.

Malcolm does not fare much better. *The Lost World* adds more depth to his character, exploring his uneasy relationship with Sarah and giving him a daughter from a previous marriage – Kelly (Vanessa Lee Chester), who stows away on the expedition.

Both complain that he is rarely there for them when they need him and accuse him of being overprotective, misguided and hypocritical in his attempts to keep them from Site B. 'If you wanted to rescue me from something, why didn't you bail me out of that fundraiser at the museum three weeks ago, like you said you would?' Sarah demands. 'Or why not rescue me from that dinner with your parents that you never showed up for? Why not rescue me when I really need it, actually be there when you say you will?' If Grant's journey in the first film is defined by his need to protect Lex and Tim, Malcolm's arc here is defined by his need to be more present in the lives of those he loves without being overbearing.

To explore this concept, Spielberg builds a bully binary around Malcolm, but his opposite is not a human character; it is the male T-Rex. Like Malcolm, the male Rex has a partner and child to look out for, and he does everything in his power to protect them. The attack on the mobile laboratory is motivated by the Rex's desire to defend its young, and a separate attack on the explorers' camp is driven by the same purpose: the Rex is monitoring the area to ensure there is no further threat. By constructing the binary in this way, Spielberg again undermines it, blurring the boundary between man and monster, hero and villain. Malcolm's behaviour is seen as a little animalistic, while the Rex is positioned as somewhat human.

With no way to easily escape the island, Malcolm is forced to spend time with Sarah and Kelly and allow them to tackle Sorna's challenges in their own way. Though she is initially scared, Kelly in particular comes to thrive in this environment, and uses her gymnastic skills to defeat a velociraptor and save her father. Sarah, meanwhile, forms a closer bond with Malcolm, one built on a greater level of mutual respect, and the third act revolves around them working together to use the juvenile Rex as bait to lure its father away from downtown San Diego. In the final scene, Malcolm, Sarah and Kelly sit in their living room, watching TV together in a perfect Spielbergian image of familial harmony.

The Rex, meanwhile, is faced with Ludlow. He has entered its cage in one last attempt to keep his dream of a new park alive and exert control over the situation. But as soon as he realises that the Rexes are also in the cage, he is reduced to a child-like state, pitifully begging the animals to 'wait' so he can escape. His pleas fall on deaf ears and he is bitten by the adult Rex, rendering him immobile. The adult does not kill him, though. Instead, he leaves that task to the infant, dragging Ludlow into his child's path and giving it the chance to learn how to kill and eat its prey without further intervention from its parent. It is every bit as happy an ending as Malcolm's, and another example of the darker approach Spielberg takes with *The Lost World*. In different ways, both the Rex and Malcolm have learned how to nurture, not simply protect, their loved ones and finish the film as better parents.

This finale also allows Spielberg to further explore The Green World and The Grey World, and show that any bond between the two has now entirely collapsed. Man and nature are in all-out war here, and Spielberg underlines this by shooting some of the most shocking violence of his career – most of which is directly associated with nature. Along with Eddie's death, we also see a palaeontologist plucked out of a waterfall and devoured, his blood pouring down the water as he is eaten. In another scene, Dieter is attacked by a pack of Compsognathus, a felled tree trunk hiding his body but not his screams, while his friend is stomped several times by the Rex, his mangled body eventually left twitching for life in the mud. In the final action on the island, many of the hunters are picked off when raptors attack them in a field of long grass. Recalling the shark moving through the water in *Jaws*, the animals slowly but surely tear through the grass, leaving tracks in their wake. Spielberg's camera looks down impassively on the devastation, his apathy representing a savage judgement on our hubris and place in the world.

Even the helping hand that the film's heroes offer results in destruction, with Sarah's attempts to heal the juvenile Rex's broken leg leading to the attack that ends in Eddie's death. Spielberg offers no second chances and very little hope in *The Lost World*. Humanity and nature are fundamentally different, their connection severed, and the film's conclusion suggests that this will be a permanent state. Indeed, the man who started the entire process insists upon its permanence. 'It is absolutely imperative that we work with the Costa Rica Department of Biological Preserves to establish a set of rules for the preservation of that island,' Hammond says in a news report. 'These creatures require our absence to survive, not our help. And if we could only step aside and trust in nature, life will find a way.'

The beautiful scenes of Sorna's dinosaurs living in isolated harmony that accompany these words provide a glimpse of what that world without humanity looks like. Tellingly for this uncommonly misanthropic Spielberg effort, they stand as one of the film's few moments of positivity.

## THESE VIOLENT DELIGHTS

*Jurassic Park* and *The Lost World* helped turn the 1990s into one of the most successful decades of Michael Crichton's career. In the same year *Jurassic Park* was released, an adaptation of Crichton's 1992 novel *Rising Sun* also hit screens, and *Disclosure* (1994), *Congo* (1995), *Sphere* (1998) and *The 13th Warrior* (1999), all derived from his novels, followed before the decade's end. Yet it was on television that Crichton found his greatest and most sustained accomplishment. Airing between 1994 and 2009, *E.R.* became a key part of American culture and won over 100 awards during its run. Crichton started the series, and his creative impulses seemed to fit the serialised format of TV better than film, which could realise his vast visual imagination, but not necessarily his rich and detailed storytelling. Only recently has it become commonplace to achieve both, with long-format 'cinematic' television delivering filmic visuals and offering enough time to explore stories to their fullest extent. Among the many projects to take advantage has been the HBO series *Westworld* (2016– ).

The show is based on the 1973 film of the same name, which Crichton both wrote and directed. Developed by Jonathan Nolan and Lisa Joy, it focuses on an elaborate theme park that is designed to resemble the Old West. Here, visitors pay a small fortune to live out their most violent and sexual fantasies without having to deal with any of the messy consequences. To enable this, the park is populated by lifelike robots (called 'hosts') who during the series come to gain autonomy, rebel against the park's controllers (a company called Delos) and escape into the real world.

It is a much more elaborate and sophisticated piece of storytelling than the original, and acts as a neat counterpoint to its view of technology. Crichton's movie is a nightmare of mechanical superiority, in which Yul Brynner's fearsome Gunslinger character pursues Richard Benjamin's naive park newcomer Peter in a fight to the death. Humanity creates machines that are stronger and smarter than we are, and we end up paying the price. Nolan and Joy's take focuses much more on humanity's inferiority and hubris. The hosts are victims not villains, the humans are their oppressors. We are still doomed, but it is our own selfish desires that seal our fate: violent delights leading to violent ends.

This is one of the show's core commonalities with *Jurassic Park* – the fallibility of Nedry, Grant and Hammond is as much to blame for the park's failure as Chaos Theory – but certainly not the only one. The two stories are also bound together by their common interest in false worlds and violent, controlling men. We hear characters speak of 'natural splendour' but know that this beauty (and the dialogue calling it beautiful) is a construct. And we follow Westworld creator Robert Ford (Anthony Hopkins) as he delights in masterminding a narrative that everyone, hosts and visitors alike, must follow to the letter, no matter how destructive it is.

More than anything, though, *Westworld* and *Jurassic Park* are linked by their interest in the way reality is perceived, even if they approach the subject in different ways. *Jurassic Park* is outward-looking and practical. It asks us to question the nature of the entertainment we consume, thereby arming us with the critical faculties needed to understand how it can affect our view of the real world. *Westworld*, however, is more inward, focusing on 'real' and 'fake' as philosophical concepts and collapsing the gap between them.

The hosts are lifelike to the finest detail and their lives are fleshed out by Ford's pre-written narratives. Yet they are not the only ones who have been programmed. As the series progresses, it is revealed that one of the park's true purposes is to capture data about its visitors. Free of consequence, guests reveal their true selves within Westworld, allowing Delos to build comprehensive profiles of who they are and how they act in certain situations. The company's terminally ill head James Delos (Peter Mullan) takes the technology even further, using it to produce an artificial version of his own consciousness that he can have transplanted into a host in order to cheat death.

With robots that look and act like humans and humans who live on as robots,

*Westworld* asks us to consider what true reality actually is, and if there is even a distinction between real and fake any more. We have dived so deep into a digital life that what makes us truly unique – memory, decision-making, love – no longer are unique. Like Hammond creating his dinosaurs, Delos wanted more; a world better than the real world, a fantasy you could 'reach out and touch' and ultimately make a lot of money from. They got what they wanted, though perhaps not with the consequences they intended. At the close of the second season, the hosts have escaped into the real world, further upsetting the delicate balance between humans and the mechanical doppelgangers we have created.

## KINGS OF THE MONSTERS

Other such delicate balances can also be found in post-*Jurassic Park* creature features. Spielberg's film helped change the way dinosaur pictures and other monster movies were seen by cinema-going audiences. By bringing dinosaurs back to life in a film that boasted revolutionary special effects, respected actors and a script that delivered real thematic weight as well as blockbuster thrills, Spielberg promoted subject matter that had previously been B-movie fodder to the A-list. But other filmmakers could not keep up with his vision or budget, and quickly reverted the genre to type.

In *Jurassic Park*'s wake, there emerged a slew of dinosaur movies that were designed to capitalise on Spielberg's hype: the likes of *Carnosaur* (1993), *Dinosaur Island* (1994), *Tammy and the T-Rex* (1994) and *Theodore Rex* (1995) took different approaches to their prehistoric stars, but were equally low in budget and quality. As the 1990s wore on, dinosaurs faded and were replaced by other monsters as the creature feature rose again in the likes of *Mimic* (1997), *Deep Rising* (1998), *Deep Blue Sea* (1999) and *Eight Legged Freaks* (2002). These boasted bigger budgets and better production values than the dinosaur pictures that preceded them, but they were either horror films with niche audiences or tongue-in-cheek parodies. Roland Emmerich's 1998 remake of *Godzilla* had the budget, the tone and the mass appeal to rival *Jurassic Park*, but it opened to poor critical notices, and so the creature feature limped into the twenty-first century with its reputation again at zero.

# CONSTELLATIONS

However, as the first century of the new millennium has developed, social and cinematic changes have conspired to bring the genre roaring back to life. Rapid advancements in home cinema technology, the success of streaming services such as Netflix and Amazon Prime and high-quality TV productions like *Westworld* have created serious competition for traditional theatrical distribution, casting doubt on the very future of cinema exhibition. Audiences no longer need to go to their local multiplex or arthouse to watch visually ambitious productions and do not have to wait long between a film's theatrical and home releases. Everything is right there for them at the touch of a button and all for a small monthly subscription fee.

To combat this threat, cinema has become grander and more event-driven. The return of 3D, rise of IMAX and continuing development of computer-generated imagery have offered filmmakers a wider and more spectacular canvas to work on, while 'universe' franchises have allowed studios to turn sequels into zeitgeist-capturing chapters in wider serialised stories. Star Wars, the DC Extended Universe and the Marvel Cinematic Universe (MCU) have taken advantage of this, but so too have creature features. Leading the way has been Legendary's 'MonsterVerse', a classic creatures series so far comprised of *Godzilla* (2014), *Kong: Skull Island* (2017) and *Godzilla: King of the Monsters* (2019), with *Godzilla vs. Kong* (2021) imminent at the time of writing. The *Jurassic Park* series has contributed too, with fourth and fifth films in the franchise arriving in 2015 (*Jurassic World*) and 2018 (*Jurassic World: Fallen Kingdom*), while the likes of *Pacific Rim* (2013) and even Spielberg's own *War of the Worlds* (2005) have offered big screen monster thrills that did not evolve into mega-franchises.

Linking this new era of the creature feature to *Jurassic Park* is its interest in nature. To varying degrees, these films comment on one of the early twenty-first century's greatest social concerns – climate change – by positioning their creatures as representations of the inevitable power of the Earth and humanity's helplessness in the face of it. The MonsterVerse, for example, portrays Godzilla as an ancient 'Titan' that is almost as old as the planet itself. Our efforts to defend ourselves against it and its battles with its various foes are seen as futile because we are essentially fighting against nature. *Pacific Rim* treads similar ground, but depicts a somewhat successful human resurgence, and *War of the Worlds* gives nature autonomy by having it (in the form of natural bacteria) fell the Martian tripods.

*Jurassic World*, meanwhile, takes the franchise's bio-engineering concept one step further than Spielberg did by introducing a hybrid animal, the Indominous Rex, which blends the DNA of several species together into one nightmare creature. In the film, directed by Colin Trevorrow, the park is now operational and has been running successfully for a number of years. However, visitors are starting to get bored of seeing the same animals time and again, and attendances are dwindling. The Indominous Rex is identified as the solution to this problem, a way to deliver something new and get people excited again. Of course, things go horribly wrong and the film places the blame at the feet of a society that destroys nature by commodifying and manipulating it. 'Twenty years ago, de-extinction was right up there with magic. These days, kids look at a stegosaurus like an elephant from the city zoo,' says the park's operations manager Claire Dearing (Bryce Dallas Howard). 'Our DNA excavators discover new species every year. But consumers want them bigger, louder – "more teeth".'

*Fallen Kingdom* reframes the franchise as a horror-tinged fairy tale. The dinosaurs are being removed from Isla Nublar before a dormant volcano eliminates them, and subsequently offered up to the black market at auction alongside another hybrid: the Indoraptor. The second half of the film is set in a grand, gothic mansion and this setting contrasts sharply with the perspective of Maisie (Isabella Sermon), an innocent young occupant of the house who idolises dinosaurs. Through this juxtaposition, director J.A. Bayona makes a definitive statement on what dinosaurs (and by extension, nature as a whole) represent. These are dream creatures that children are fascinated by and who put them in touch with something extraordinary. The rebirth of the dinosaurs and creation of the Indominous Rex and Indoraptor compromises that purity, turning the dream into a nightmare. The only way to restore their position is to release them into the wild, which Maisie does at the film's end.

Its final moments see the dinosaurs interacting with the modern world: a mosasaur readies itself to devour a surfer, a T-Rex squares up against a lion, a raptor stands on the edges of a suburban town. It brings the franchise full circle – what began as man encroaching on nature concludes with nature encroaching on man – and is portrayed as somewhat triumphant, something to be celebrated. To put it in Spielbergian terms *Fallen Kingdom*, like *Jurassic Park, The Lost World, Westworld* and so many modern creature features, establishes the dominance of The Grey World as a threat and suggests that The Green World's violent resurgence may be the only thing that can save us.

Control is lost. Chaos reigns. A butterfly flaps its wings and man is powerless to resist.

# WORKS CITED

Baxter, J. (1997) *Steven Spielberg: The Unauthorised Biography*. New York: Harper Collins Publishing.

Bouzereau, Laurent. 'Lawrence of Arabia: A Conversation With Steven Spielberg'. Columbia TriStar Home Entertainment, 2000.

Bouzereau, Laurent. 'Return to Jurassic Park'. Universal Studios Home Video, 2011.

Browne, M.W. 'In New Spielberg Film, A Dim View of Science.' *The New York Times*, 11 May 1993.

Brubaker, P. (2017) 'Spielberg/Suspense'. Fandor. https://youtu.be/tQ5XB9eDVM4 (Accessed 9 December 2017).

Cohen, C. (2010) *Masters of Cinema: Steven Spielberg*. Paris: Cahiers du Cinéma.

Collins, G. (1985). 'Spielberg Films The Color Purple'. *New York Times*. Reprinted in *Steven Spielberg Interviews*. Eds. Lester D. Friedman and Brent Notbohm. Jackson: University of Mississippi Press, 2000.

Corliss, R. 'What's Old is Gold: A Triumph for Indy 3.' *Time*. 29 May 1989.

Crawley, T. (1983) *The Steven Spielberg Story*. London: Zomba Books.

Crichton, M. (1991) *Jurassic Park*. London: Arrow Books.

Crichton, M. (1993) in 'Making Jurassic Park'. *Starburst: Dinosaur Special* (Issue 17). August 1993.

Dick, P.K. (1990) *Paycheck and Other Classic Stories by Philip K. Dick*. New York: Citadel Press Books.

Dubner, S.J. (1999) 'Steven the Good.' *New York Times Magazine*. Reprinted in *Steven Spielberg Interviews*. Eds. Lester D. Friedman and Brent Notbohm. Jackson: University of Mississippi Press, 2000.

Ebert, R. and Siskel, G. (1991) *The Future of Movies: Interviews with Martin Scorsese, Steven Spielberg and George Lucas*. Kansas City: Andrews and McMeel.

Ebert, R. and Siskel, G. 'Siskel and Ebert: The Future of Movies.' 21 May 1990.

Forsberg, M. (1988) 'Spielberg at 40: The Man and the Child'. New York Times. Reprinted in *Steven Spielberg Interviews*. Eds. Lester D. Friedman and Brent Notbohm. Jackson: University of Mississippi Press, 2000.

Freer, I. 'The Game Changer'. *Empire Magazine*. April 2018.

Freer, I. (2015) 'Steven, Have They Figured Out What I'm Looking Up In Awe At Yet? How SFX Became The Director's Lifeline', *empireonline.com* (online). https://www.empireonline.com/movies/features/steven-spielberg-special-effects/ (Accessed 10 December 2017)

Friedman, L.D. and Notbohm, B. (eds) (2000) *Steven Spielberg Interviews*. Jackson: University of Mississippi Press.

Goldenberg, A. (2015) 'Close Encounters of the Steven Spielberg Kind in Arizona', Forward.com (online). https://forward.com/culture/305981/close-encounters-of-the-arizona-kind/ (Accessed 25 November 2017).

Gordon, A.M. (2008) *Empire of Dreams: The Science Fiction Films of Steven Spielberg*. Lanham: Rowman and Littlefield.

Kakutani, M. 'The Two Faces of Spielberg: Horror v Hope. *New York Times*. 30 May 1982.

Kermode, M. and Mayo, S. (2013) 'Steven Spielberg Interview', BBC Radio Five Live (online). https://youtu.be/cnwQDgssrwk (Accessed 26 November 2017).

Kincaid, P. (2003) 'On the Origins of Genre'. *Speculations on Speculation: Theories of Science Fiction*. Lanham: The Scarecrow Press.

Koresky, M. (2012) 'The Greenhouse Effect.' Reverse Shot (online). http://reverseshot.org/archive/entry/757/always (Accessed 12 November 2017).

Lacy, S. 'Spielberg'. HBO Documentary Films, Pentimento Productions, 2017.

Lee, K.B. (2011) 'The Spielberg Face'. Fandor (online). https://vimeo.com/199572277 (Accessed 25 November 2017).

Lewis, A. (2015) 'How Steven Spielberg's Cold War Childhood Inspired Bridge of Spies.' *The Hollywood Reporter* (online) https://www.hollywoodreporter.com/features/how-steven-spielbergs-cold-war-840896 (Accessed 12th November 2017).

Lister, D. (1993) 'Jurassic Park Given PG Rating: Censors Warn Parents of "Disturbing Scenes".' *The Independent* (online). https://www.independent.co.uk/news/uk/jurassic-park-given-pg-rating-censors-warn-parents-of-disturbing-scenes-1493077.html (Accessed 12 November 2017).

Mars-Jones, A. (1993) 'Spare the Rod, Spoil the Child.' *The Independent* (online). https://www.independent.co.uk/arts-entertainment/film-the-big-picture-spare-the-rod-spoil-the-child-adam-mars-jones-reviews-steven-spielbergs-1485156.html (Accessed 12 November 2017).

Maslin, J. (1993) 'Screen Stars With Teeth to Spare.' *The New York Times* (online). https://www.nytimes.com/1993/06/11/movies/review-film-screen-stars-with-teeth-to-spare.html (Accessed 12 November 2017).

McBride, J. (2010) *Steven Spielberg: A Biography* (Second Edition). University Press of Mississippi.

McCarthy, T. (1993) 'Jurassic Park.' *Variety* (online). https://variety.com/1993/film/reviews/jurassic-park-2-1200432562/ (Accessed 12 November 2017).

Morris, N. (2007) *Empire of Light: The Cinema of Steven Spielberg*. London: Wallflower Press.

Nathan, I. 'The Terminal.' *Empire Magazine*. October 2004.

Pirie, D. 'A Prodigy Zooms In: A Child Cineaste Who Now Makes Movies and Money With Equal Facility'. *Time Out*. 10 November 1978.

Podrazik, J. (2012). 'Spielberg on Spielberg: "I Have A Lot More Patience Than I Ever Gave Myself Credit For".' *The Huffington Post* (online). https://www.huffpost.com/entry/spielberg-on-spielberg-dicaprio-oprah-lincoln_n_2303915 (Accessed 12 November 2017).

Pramaggiore, M. and Wallis, T. (2005) *Film: A Critical Introduction*. London: Laurence King Publishing.

Provencher, K. (2016) 'The Spielberg Touchscreen'. Vimeo (online). https://vimeo.com/151984751 (Accessed 10 December 2017).

Schleier, C. (1994). 'Steven Spielberg's New Direction'. *Jewish Monthly* 108, no. 4 (January/February 1994).

Schultz, J. 'The Making of Jurassic Park'. Amblin Entertainment, Les Mayfield Productions and Zaloom Mayfield Productions, 1995.

Shandler, J.A. (1997) 'Schindler's Discourse: America Discusses the Holocaust and its Mediation, from NBC's Miniseries to Spielberg's Film.' *Spielberg's Holocaust Critical Perspectives on Schindler's List*. Ed Yosefa Loshitzky. Bloomington: Indiana University Press.

Shay, D. and Duncan, J. (1993) *The Making of Jurassic Park*. Great Britain: Boxtree.

Sragow, M. (1982) 'A Conversation With Steven Spielberg.' *Rolling Stone*. Reprinted in *Steven Spielberg Interviews*. Eds. Lester D. Friedman and Brent Notbohm. Jackson: University of Mississippi Press, 2000.

Taylor, P.M. (1992) *Steven Spielberg*. London: B.T. Batsford.

Tinius, A. (2017) 'Spielberg: How to Introduce Characters'. Entertain the Elk (online). https://youtu.be/iQLJDxp2FEI (Accessed 10 December 2017).

Turner, G.E. (1983) 'Flashback: Steven Spielberg and E.T.: The Extra-Terrestrial. *American Cinematographer* (online). https://ascmag.com/articles/spielberg-et-the-extraterrestrial (Accessed 10 December 2017).

Tuchman, M. (1978). 'Close Encounter with Steven Spielberg'. *Film Comment*. Reprinted in *Steven Spielberg Interviews*. Eds. Lester D. Friedman and Brent Notbohm. Jackson: University of Mississippi Press, 2000.

Vincent, M. (2015) 'Tom Hanks and Steven Spielberg on Film, History and the "Battle for Civilisation".' ABC News (online). https://youtu.be/aZ7IVsMaLXs (Accessed 12 November 2017).

Wasser, F. (2010) *Steven Spielberg's America*. Cambridge: Polity Press.

Willems, P.H. (2017) 'Steven Spielberg and the Horror Inside Blockbusters.' YouTube (online). https://youtu.be/YWqyNE6ok14 (Accessed 12 November 2017).

Zhou, T. (2014) 'The Spielberg Oner'. Every Frame A Painting (online). https://youtu.be/8q4X2vDRfRk (Accessed 10 December 2017).

'The Life of Film's Living Legend Steven Spielberg'. CNN (online transcript of an interview aired 23 June 2001). http://transcripts.cnn.com/TRANSCRIPTS/0106/23/pitn.00.html (Accessed 13 January 2018).

'The Summer of the Shark.' *Time*. 23 June 1975. http://content.time.com/time/magazine/article/0,9171,913189,00.html (Accessed 9 December 2017).